microwave cooking library™

microwaving convenience foods

by barbara methven

microwave cooking library ™·

Microwave oven owners are busy people. Their active lives leave them little time to cook. Many of them belong to the growing number of American consumers who use convenience foods. The microwave oven gives them an added advantage, making convenience products even more convenient.

This book was written in response to consumer requests for more information on how to microwave convenience foods and use these products creatively. The recipe sections approach convenience foods as ingredients with which you can cook a wealth of new dishes without sacrificing convenience or time-saving. The second section of the book provides comprehensive charts and step-by-step directions for microwaving canned, frozen, refrigerated or take-out foods and dry mixes.

Microwaving Convenience Foods shows you how to combine microwave speed with convenience products and introduces you to a wide variety of new and different dishes you can prepare in minutes.

Barbara Methven

Barbara Methven

CREDITS:
Design & Production: Cy DeCosse Creative Department, Inc.
Consultant: Joanne Crocker
Art Director: Delores Swanson
Production Coordinators: Mary Ann Knox, Christine Watkins
Photographers: Buck Holzemer, Michael Jensen, Ken Greer
Food Stylists: Suzanne Finley, Maria Rolandelli, Lynn Lohmann,
  Carol Grones, Susan Zechmann
Home Economists: Peggy Lamb, Susan Zechmann,
  Maureen Mortinson, Jill Crum
Consumer Testers: Linda Lea Stearns, Judith Richard,
  Anne Antolak, Barbara Kirby
Typesetting: Ellen Sorenson
Color Separations: Weston Engraving Co., Inc.
Printing: R. R. Donnelley & Sons Company

Additional volumes in the Microwave Cooking Library series are available from the publisher:

- Basic Microwaving
- Recipe Conversion for Microwave
- Microwaving Meats
- Microwave Baking & Desserts
- Microwaving Meals in 30 Minutes
- Microwaving on a Diet
- Microwaving Fruits & Vegetables
- Microwaving for Holidays & Parties
- Microwave Cooking for One & Two
- The Microwave & Freezer
- 101 Microwaving Secrets

Contents

What You Need to Know Before You Start

Americans have been using convenience foods for over one hundred years. Some convenience foods have become such a day-to-day part of our lives that they are used more frequently than foods prepared "from scratch." Examples are canned soups and cake mixes, which also appear as ingredients in other home-cooked dishes.

Convenience foods and the microwave oven are natural partners. Both are time savers. When the foods are microwaved, convenience is maximized. Almost all convenience foods can be prepared by microwaving. This book tells you how to convert conventional package directions and how to use convenience foods in exciting new recipes.

To allow for the possibility of new, reformulated and discontinued products, this book lists only generic product names. To find products in the charts of basic directions, you will have to think in terms of what the product contains rather than its brand name. When using the index, look for main ingredient categories (i.e. noodles) or for general groups (i.e. side dish).

How to Use This Book

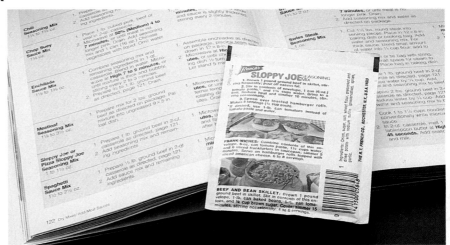

Recipes Using Convenience Foods

Today's busy homemakers use and enjoy convenience foods, but they still like to give their meals a personal touch. The recipe section of this book approaches convenience foods as ingredients for "home made" foods. There are quick ideas for dressing up and varying convenience foods, as well as recipes which combine several convenience items to produce a new, but still convenient dish.

Converting Package Directions for Microwave

The second section of the book provides step-by-step directions and charts for the basic microwaving of convenience foods.

Use the package as a guide, but refer to the charts for ingredient adjustments and microwave times.

Many convenience products have microwave directions on the package. Look for them, and use the instructions in this book as a complement to the information provided by the food manufacturer.

The charts are organized like the sections in your supermarket — canned goods, frozen foods, refrigerated foods, dry mixes and deli foods.

All foods in the charts are available nationwide. Many other convenience foods are available in local distribution or in test markets. You can also microwave these by following the basic microwaving directions for a similar product.

Making the Most of Convenience Foods

The primary purpose of convenience products is to make your cooking easier. Some are already prepared, while others simplify the preparation of dishes which are time consuming or need a practiced hand to make.

As you'll learn from the recipes in this book, the use of convenience products is not limited to the package directions. They can serve as shortcut ingredients in new dishes, to combine convenience and creative cooking. These sample menus are planned from the recipes and illustrate the variety possible.

The following lists for pantry, refrigerator, and freezer are composed of products used often in the recipes or to give convenience cooking a personal touch. Most of them are not main ingredients, which you would buy when you plan to make a dish, although the list includes items to keep on hand for emergencies. Some are products you already have and use frequently. With others, the possibility of using them as ingredients may not have occurred to you. The list can serve as a guide to expanding your use of convenience foods.

Convenience Ingredients to Keep on Hand

Canned Foods

Broth: beef, chicken
Chicken, chunked
Chili
Crab meat
Dried beef
Evaporated milk
French fried onion rings
Gravy
Ham, chunked
Mushrooms
Pie fillings
Salmon
Shoestring potatoes
Soups: cream of mushroom
  cream of chicken, tomato
Sweetened condensed milk
Tomatoes
Tuna
Vegetables

Dry Products

Bread crumbs
Buttermilk baking mix
Cake mixes
Chocolate chips
Croutons
Dried chives
Gelatin
Graham cracker crumbs
Gravy mixes
Herb stuffing mix
Hot roll mix
Instant beverage mixes
Instant bouillon granules
Instant mashed potatoes
Instant minced onion
Onion soup mix
Pudding mix
Rolled oats
Sauce mixes: white, cheese,
  hollandaise

Frozen Foods

Bread dough: loaves and
  dinner rolls
Chives
Fruit: raspberries,
  strawberries
Green pepper, chopped
Onion, chopped
Pie shell
Vegetables
Whipped topping

Refrigerated Foods

Bacon
Barbecue sauce
Cheese: cream, grated,
  shredded slices, processed
  spread, processed loaf
Dairy sour cream
Ham: canned, slices
Hot dogs

Sample Menus

Breakfast

Pictured bottom:
Ham & Cheese Omelet, page 45
Apple-Nut Pull Aparts, page 69
Bacon Strips or Sausage Patties, page 148

Bacon & Egg Sandwich, page 47
Mocha Chocolate, page 19

Lunch

Pictured upper left:
Hamburger Vegetable Soup, page 23
Frozen Bran Muffins, page 103

Chili Beef Soup, page 23
Mexican Muffins, page 71
Peanut Butter Snack Cake, page 74

Double Cheese Macaroni & Cheese, page 47
Hot Ham Sandwich, page 26
Tossed Salad

Dinner

Pictured upper right:
Shrimp Newburg, page 37
Frozen Asparagus Spears, page 99
Tossed Salad
Raspberry Peach Compote, page 78

Chunky Beef Stew & Biscuits, page 29
Tossed Salad
Coffee Pecan Ice Cream Pie, page 77

Oriental Soup, page 22
Curried Egg Foo Yung, page 46
Fried Rice, page 42

Saucy Fried Chicken, page 34
Mexicali Corn Casserole, page 57
Tossed Salad
Sour Cream Pineapple Pie, page 77

Spaghetti, page 32
Cheese French Bread, page 65
Tossed Salad

Appetizers

The ingredients for many tasty appetizers can be kept on hand and stirred together at a moment's notice. Use these convenient appetizers to introduce a party, dress up a family dinner, or serve as a light meal on a warm summer day.

◄ Spinach Dip

2 pkgs. (10 oz. each) frozen
    chopped spinach
1 pkg. (1⅝ oz.) dry vegetable
    soup mix without noodles
½ cup water

1 pkg. (8 oz.) cream cheese
1 cup (8 oz.) dairy sour cream
    with chives
5 to 6 drops red pepper
    sauce, optional

Makes 4 cups

To defrost spinach, place packages in oven. Microwave at High 4 minutes, turning packages over after half the time. Let stand 5 minutes. Drain thoroughly. Set aside.

Place soup mix and water in small bowl. Cover with plastic wrap. Microwave at High 1 minute. Let stand, covered, until vegetables are rehydrated.

Place cream cheese in large bowl. Reduce power to 50% (Medium). Microwave 1 minute to soften. Mix in rehydrated soup mix, drained spinach, sour cream and red pepper sauce. Serve with sour dough or French bread cubes, carrot sticks or crackers, if desired.

Sour Cream Bean Dip

1 can (17 oz.) refried beans
½ cup dairy sour cream
½ cup red salsa sauce
¼ cup finely chopped green
    onions, or 2 tablespoons
    dried chives
1 medium tomato, chopped,
    optional
½ cup shredded Cheddar
    cheese

Makes 3 cups

In 2-qt. casserole combine beans, sour cream, salsa sauce and green onions. Microwave at 70% (Medium-High) 5 to 8 minutes, or until heated, stirring every 2 minutes. Stir in chopped tomato. Sprinkle with cheese. Microwave at 70% (Medium-High) 1 to 2 minutes, or until cheese is melted. Serve with taco chips, corn chips, or rolled flour tortillas, if desired.

Chili Cheese Dip

pictured on page 9

1 pkg. (16 oz.) processed
    cheese loaf, cut into
    1-in. cubes
1 can (4 oz.) chopped green
    chilies
1 can (15 oz.) hot chili with
    or without beans

Makes 3 cups

Place all ingredients in 2-qt. casserole. Microwave at 50% (Medium) 12 to 15 minutes, or until cheese is melted, stirring every 3 to 4 minutes. Garnish with shredded lettuce, or chopped green onions, tomato, or black olives, if desired. Serve with corn or taco chips.

Variation:
Prepare as directed and spoon over hot dogs.

Hot Peppered Crab Dip

1 pkg. (8 oz.) cream cheese
1 cup dairy sour cream with
    chives
1 can (5 to 6½ oz.) crab meat,
    drained, cartilage removed
1 teaspoon dried onion flakes
⅛ teaspoon cayenne pepper

Makes 2½ cups

Place cream cheese in 1½- to
2-qt. casserole. Microwave at
50% (Medium) 1 to 1½ minutes,
or until softened. Stir in remaining ingredients. Increase power
to 70% (Medium-High).
Microwave 4 to 6 minutes, or
until heated, stirring after half
the cooking time. Serve with
crackers or chips, if desired.

Hot Chipped Beef Dip

1 pkg. (8 oz.) cream cheese
1 cup dairy sour cream
1 jar (2½ oz.) dried beef,
    rinsed with hot water,
    drained and snipped
⅛ to ¼ teaspoon red pepper,
    optional

Makes 2 cups

Place cream cheese in 1- to
1½-qt. casserole or serving
dish. Microwave at 50%
(Medium) 1 to 1½ minutes, or
until softened. Blend in sour
cream, beef and red pepper.

Microwave at 50% (Medium)
3 to 5 minutes, or until heated,
stirring after every 2 minutes.
Serve with crackers or chips,
if desired.

Variation:
Sprinkle dip with ¼ cup
chopped walnuts or pecans.

Orange Barbecue ▲ Cocktail Weiners

2 cups bottled barbecue sauce
1 jar (10 oz.) orange
    marmalade
¼ to ½ teaspoon dry mustard
1 pkg. (1 lb.) hot dogs,
    quartered and butterflied

Makes 1 qt.

In 2-qt. casserole combine
barbecue sauce, marmalade
and mustard. Stir in hot dogs;
cover. Microwave at High 5 to
8 minutes, or until hot, stirring
every 2 minutes.

Seasoned Spinach Balls ▲

1 pkg. (10 oz.) frozen
    chopped spinach
¼ cup butter or margarine
2 eggs
1½ cups herb-seasoned
    stuffing mix
½ cup shredded Cheddar
    cheese
2 cups grated Parmesan
    cheese
⅛ teaspoon garlic powder

Makes 24 appetizers

To defrost spinach, place package in oven. Microwave at High 3
to 4 minutes, or until defrosted, turning package over after half the
time. Drain thoroughly. Set aside.

Place butter in small dish. Microwave at High 1 to 1½ minutes, or
until melted. Set aside. In medium bowl beat eggs slightly. Stir in
remaining ingredients, adding melted butter last. Shape by
spoonfuls into 24 balls. Arrange in 12 × 8-in. baking dish. Cover
with wax paper. Reduce power to 70% (Medium-High). Microwave
5 to 7 minutes, or until firm to the touch, rotating dish after half the
cooking time.

Party Reubens ▲

12 slices cocktail rye bread
  Thousand Island dressing or
  sandwich spread
1 pkg. (2½ oz.) fully cooked
  pressed corned beef

1 can (8 oz.) sauerkraut, well
  drained
2 slices Swiss cheese, each
  cut into 6 pieces

Makes 12 appetizers

Toast bread slices under broiler. Spread toasted side of each with
small amount of dressing. Arrange in paper towel-lined 12 × 8-in.
baking dish. Layer each with a slice of corned beef, folded to fit, a
generous teaspoon of sauerkraut and a piece of cheese. Press
lightly with fingers. Microwave at High 2 to 3 minutes, or until
sandwich is hot and cheese melts, rotating dish after half the
cooking time.

Shrimp & Pineapple ▲

1 bottle (8 oz.) French dressing
1 can (8¼ oz.) pineapple
  chunks
1 pkg. (10 oz.) ready-to-cook
  frozen cocktail shrimp,
  defrosted*

Serves 8 to 10

In 2-qt. casserole combine
dressing, pineapple with juice
and shrimp; cover. Microwave
at 50% (Medium) 9 to 11 minutes, or until shrimp are
opaque, stirring every 3 minutes. Do not overcook. Let
stand, covered, 5 minutes.
Serve hot or chilled.

*Defrost shrimp under cold
running water.

◄ Apricot-Sausage Kabobs

  1 pkg. (8 oz.) fully cooked
     sausage links
  1 can (16 to 17 oz.) apricot
     halves, drained and ¾ cup
     juice reserved
¼ cup soy sauce
  2 tablespoons packed brown
     sugar
  1 can (15½ oz.) pineapple
     chunks, drained
30 sandwich picks

          Makes 30 kabobs

Cut sausages into thirds. In
small bowl combine reserved
apricot juice, soy sauce and
brown sugar. Stir in sausage
pieces. Let stand 5 minutes.

Cut apricot halves in half. Drain
sausages, reserving sauce.
Alternate apricot, sausage and
pineapple pieces on each
sandwich pick. Arrange about
15 kabobs on microwave
roasting rack. Brush generously
with sauce. Microwave at High
4 to 5 minutes, or until heated,
rotating rack, turning kabobs
over and basting with sauce
after half the cooking time.
Repeat with remaining kabobs.

◄ Barbecued
Shoestring Potatoes

½ cup butter or margarine
  1 pkg. (1½ oz.) barbecue
     sauce mix or 2 pkgs.
     (1¼ oz. each) sour cream
     sauce mix
  1 can (14 oz.) shoestring
     potatoes

          Makes 14 cups

Place butter in 2-cup measure.
Microwave at High 1 to 1½
minutes, or until melted. Stir in
sauce mix. Place shoestring
potatoes in large bowl. Pour
butter mixture over potatoes,
tossing to coat. Microwave at
High 4 to 6 minutes, or until
heated, stirring every 2 minutes.
Let stand 5 minutes.

Cheese Pastry Straws

1 pkg. (11 oz.) pie crust mix
1 envelope (1¼ oz.) cheese
  sauce mix
1 tablespoon real bacon bits
⅛ teaspoon chili powder,
  optional
5 to 6 tablespoons very cold
  water

Makes 5½ to 6 dozen

How to Microwave Cheese Pastry Straws

Mix pie crust mix, cheese sauce mix, bacon bits and chili powder in medium bowl. Sprinkle with water, while tossing with a fork, until pastry holds together.

Divide pastry in half; shape into smooth balls. Roll out to ⅛-in. thickness on lightly floured board. Cut into 1 × 3-in. strips. Repeat with remaining pastry.

Line microwave baking sheet or 12 × 12-in. sheet of cardboard with wax paper. Arrange about 2 dozen sticks on sheet. Place in oven on inverted saucer.

Microwave at High 2 to 4 minutes, or until dry and puffy, rotating ¼ turn after half the cooking time. Watch closely to prevent burning. Remove to serving plate. Cool completely.

15

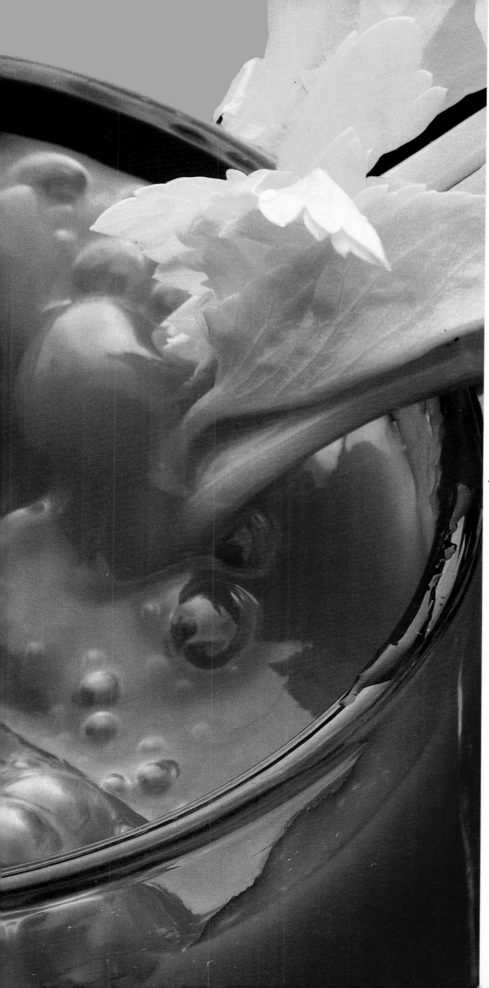

Beverages

Add seasonings to beverage mixes or combine canned, frozen or instant beverages to create special drinks. Provide extra appeal with a simple garnish such as celery stalk or green onion.

◄ Zippy Tomato Drink

1 can (46 oz.) vegetable cocktail juice
1 tablespoon Worcestershire sauce
8 to 10 drops red pepper sauce
½ teaspoon celery salt

Serves 6

In 2-qt. casserole combine all ingredients; cover. Microwave at High 10 to 14 minutes, or until heated, stirring after half the cooking time. Garnish with celery stick or lemon wedge, if desired.

Hot Chocolate

1 cup milk
Chocolate syrup

Serves 1

Measure milk into serving mug or 1-cup measure. Microwave at High 1½ to 2 minutes, or until heated. Stir in chocolate syrup to taste.

Sunny Tea ▲

¼ cup instant lemon-flavored
    tea powder
2 tablespoons packed brown
    sugar
½ teaspoon ground cinnamon
¼ teaspoon ground nutmeg

5 cups hot water
1 can (6 oz.) frozen pine-
    apple-orange juice
    concentrate, defrosted as
    directed, page 104

Serves 6

In 2-qt. casserole combine tea, brown sugar, cinnamon and
nutmeg. Gradually stir in water. Add concentrate; cover. Microwave at High 8 to 10 minutes, or until heated, stirring after half the
cooking time. Garnish with lemon slices, if desired.

Hot Punch ▲

1 jar (32 oz.) cranberry-apple
    drink
¼ cup packed brown sugar
1 tablespoon lemon juice
4 whole cloves
2 cinnamon sticks
1 cup red wine, optional

Serves 6

In 2-qt. casserole combine all
ingredients except wine; cover.
Microwave at High 6 to 8
minutes, or until heated, stirring
after half the cooking time and
adding wine when 2 minutes
cooking time remain.

Mocha Chocolate ▲

½ cup instant cocoa mix
¼ cup instant coffee crystals
4 cups hot water

Serves 4

Combine instant cocoa and coffee. Measure water into 2-qt. measure; cover. Microwave at High 5 to 8 minutes, or until almost boiling. Stir in cocoa and coffee mixture. Pour into serving cups. Garnish with whipped topping and shaved chocolate curls, if desired.

Hot Beef Broth ▲

2 cans (10½ oz. each)
   condensed beef broth
1¾ cups hot water
1½ teaspoons lemon juice
1 teaspoon Worcestershire
   sauce

½ teaspoon prepared
   horseradish
2 to 4 tablespoons sherry,
   optional
4 green onions

Serves 4

In 2-qt. casserole combine broth, water, lemon juice, Worcestershire sauce and horseradish; cover. Microwave at High 6 to 8 minutes, or until heated, stirring after half the cooking time. Mix in sherry. Pour into serving cups. Serve with whole green onions.

Soups & Sandwiches

Sandwich fillings and soups are among the most frequently used convenience foods. Manufacturers provide good variety, but you needn't stop there. By combining a few items from the pantry, refrigerator or freezer you can create new soups and sandwiches with ease.

◀ Beer Cheese Soup

¼ cup butter or margarine
½ cup all-purpose flour
2 tablespoons instant onion flakes
1 can (13 oz.) evaporated milk
1 cup milk
1 jar (16 oz.) cheese food spread
1 can (12 oz.) beer

Serves 6

Place butter in 3-qt. casserole. Microwave at High 30 to 60 seconds, or until melted. Blend in flour and onion flakes. Add evaporated milk and milk, one-third at a time, blending after each addition. Microwave at High 5 to 7 minutes, or until hot, bubbly and thickened, stirring after the first 2 minutes and then after each minute.

Stir in cheese until cheese melts and mixture is smooth. Blend in beer. Microwave at High 1 to 2 minutes, or until desired serving temperature. Garnish individual servings with popcorn or pretzels, if desired.

Pictured: Hot Chicken Sandwich

French Onion Soup

2 cans (10½ oz. each)
    condensed onion soup
1 can (10¾ oz.) condensed
    chicken broth
2 cups water
2 tablespoons butter or
    margarine
¼ teaspoon dry mustard
    Dash pepper
3 French or hard rolls, halved
    and toasted
1½ cups shredded Swiss
    cheese
3 tablespoons grated
    Parmesan cheese

Serves 6

In 3-qt. casserole combine onion soup, chicken broth, water, butter, mustard and pepper; cover. Microwave at High 6 to 9 minutes, or until heated, stirring after half the time.

Ladle soup into six serving bowls. Top each with toasted roll, ¼ cup Swiss cheese and 1½ teaspoons Parmesan. Place 4 bowls in oven. Microwave at High 2 to 3 minutes, or until heated and cheese melts, rearranging bowls after half the time. Microwave remaining 2 bowls at High 1 to 2 minutes.

Oriental Soup ▲

1 can (10¾ oz.) condensed
    chicken broth
1 can (10½ oz.) condensed
    chicken with rice soup
1 pkg. (10 oz.) frozen stir-fry
    vegetables with seasoning
2 cups hot water
1 can (4 oz.) mushroom stems
    and pieces, drained

Serves 6

Combine all ingredients, including vegetable seasoning packet, in 3-qt. casserole; cover. Microwave at High 8 to 10 minutes, or until hot, stirring 2 or 3 times during cooking.

Hot Vichyssoise

2 cups prepared instant
    mashed potatoes (4
    servings), page 131
1 can (13 oz.) evaporated milk
2 tablespoons butter or
    margarine
1 teaspoon instant chicken
    bouillon granules
1 teaspoon dried chives
½ teaspoon onion powder
¼ teaspoon celery salt

Serves 4

Mix all ingredients in 2-qt. casserole until smooth. Microwave at High 4 to 6 minutes, or until hot and bubbly, stirring once or twice.

Borscht

1 container (6¾ oz.) starter for
    beef barley soup
6 cups hot water
1 can (16 oz.) shoestring
    beets, drained and
    juice reserved
2 tablespoons lemon juice
⅛ teaspoon ground allspice

Serves 4 to 6

In 3-qt. casserole combine starter ingredients, water, reserved beet juice, lemon juice and allspice; cover. Microwave at High 20 to 30 minutes, or until vegetables are rehydrated, stirring every 10 minutes. Stir in beets. Top each serving with sour cream, if desired.

Hamburger Vegetable Soup

1 lb. ground beef
1 tablespoon instant minced onion
4 cups hot water
1 pkg. (16 oz.) frozen mixed vegetables
1 can (16 oz.) sliced potatoes, drained
1 can (12 oz.) vegetable cocktail juice
1 can (10½ oz.) condensed beef broth
1 to 2 teaspoons salt
1 bay leaf
¼ teaspoon ground marjoram

Serves 6 to 8

Crumble ground beef in 4- to 5-qt. casserole. Add instant onion. Microwave at High 4 to 5 minutes, or until meat is no longer pink, stirring to break up meat after half the time. Drain.

Stir in remaining ingredients; cover. Microwave at High 8 to 10 minutes. Stir. Reduce power to 50% (Medium). Microwave 20 to 25 minutes, or until soup is hot and flavors are blended, stirring once or twice during cooking. Let stand, covered, 5 to 10 minutes.

Cream of Broccoli Soup

1 pkg. (10 oz.) frozen broccoli cuts
1 can (10¾ oz.) condensed cream of mushroom soup
1½ cups milk
½ cup water
1 teaspoon dried chives
⅛ teaspoon pepper
Dash nutmeg

Serves 4

Microwave broccoli in box at High 3 to 5 minutes, or until defrosted. Chop finely. In 2-qt. casserole mix broccoli and remaining ingredients; cover. Microwave at High 6 to 12 minutes, or until heated, stirring 2 or 3 times. Top with dairy sour cream, if desired.

Chili Beef Soup ▲

1 can (15 oz.) chili without beans
1 can (15 oz.) kidney beans, drained
1 can (10¾ oz.) condensed tomato soup
1 cup water
½ cup frozen chopped green pepper
¼ to ½ teaspoon chili powder

Serves 6

Combine all ingredients in 2-qt. casserole; cover. Microwave at High 8 to 10 minutes, or until heated, stirring 2 or 3 times during cooking.

Corn Chowder

1 can (10¾ oz.) cream of potato soup
1 can (17 oz.) creamed corn
1 soup can half and half
1 soup can milk

Serves 4 to 6

Combine all ingredients in 2-qt. casserole. Cover. Microwave at High 5 to 9 minutes, or until heated, stirring 2 or 3 times during cooking.

◄ Seafood Bisque

1 can (11 oz.) condensed
   tomato bisque soup
1 can (10¾ oz.) condensed
   cream of shrimp soup
1½ cups milk
1 to 2 tablespoons sherry or
   white wine
Dash cayenne pepper
1 can (5 to 6½ oz.) crab
   meat, rinsed, drained
   and cartilage removed

Serves 4

In 2-qt. casserole combine soups, milk, sherry and cayenne pepper; cover. Microwave at High 5 to 6 minutes, or until heated, stirring after half the time. Mix in crab meat. Microwave at High 1 to 2 minutes, or until of desired temperature.

New Soups From Two Soups

In 2-qt. casserole dilute soup combinations, below, with 2 soup cans of liquid. Use hot water, milk or a combination of both. For a richer, creamier soup dilute with 1 soup can milk and 1 soup can half and half, or use 1 can (13 oz.) evaporated milk and ¼ cup hot water. For extra zest, stir in 1 tablespoon dried onion flakes or 1 to 2 teaspoons dried chives. Add salt and pepper, if desired.

Microwave, covered, at High 5 to 9 minutes, or until heated, stirring 2 or 3 times during cooking.

Soup Combinations

Cheddar Asparagus Soup
  1 can (10¾ oz.) condensed cream of asparagus soup
  1 can (11 oz.) condensed Cheddar cheese soup

Clam & Potato Chowder
  1 can (10¾ oz.) condensed New England clam chowder
  1 can (10¾ oz.) condensed cream of potato soup

Creamy Chicken Vegetable Soup
  1 can (10¾ oz.) condensed cream of chicken soup
  1 can (10¾ oz.) condensed chicken vegetable soup

Bean, Pea & Pork Soup
  1 can (11½ oz.) condensed split pea with ham soup
  1 can (11½ oz.) condensed bean with bacon soup

Hearty Chowder
  1 can (10¾ oz.) condensed New England clam chowder
  1 can (10¾ oz.) condensed tomato soup

Individual Pizzas ▲

1 can (10½ oz.) pizza sauce
6 English muffins, halved
   and toasted
1 pkg. (2½ to 3½ oz.)
   thin-sliced pepperoni
1 can (4 oz.) mushroom
   stems and pieces, drained
1½ cups shredded mozzarella
   cheese

Serves 6

Spread 1 tablespoon pizza
sauce on each muffin half. Top
each with 3 slices pepperoni
and 3 or 4 mushroom pieces.
Sprinkle with 2 tablespoons
mozzarella cheese. Add grated
Parmesan cheese, chopped
onion and chopped black or
green olives, if desired.

Place 6 muffin halves on paper
towel-lined plate. Microwave at
High 1½ to 2 minutes, or until
cheese melts, rotating plate ½
turn after half the cooking time.
Repeat with remaining muffins.

Crab Bagels

2 pkgs. (3 oz. each) cream
   cheese with chives
1 can (5 to 6½ oz.) crab meat,
   rinsed, drained and
   cartilage removed
2 tablespoons frozen chopped
   green pepper
1 teaspoon lemon juice
½ teaspoon Worcestershire
   sauce
4 bagels, halved and toasted
   Paprika, optional

Serves 4

Place cream cheese in 1-qt.
casserole. Microwave at 50%
(Medium) 1 to 1½ minutes, or
until softened. Stir in crab meat,
green pepper, lemon juice and
Worcestershire sauce.

Spread about 3 tablespoons
crab mixture on each bagel
half. Sprinkle with paprika.
Arrange 4 sandwiches on paper
towel-lined plate. Microwave at
High 1 to 1½ minutes, or until
heated, rotating plate ½ turn
after half the cooking time.
Sprinkle with paprika. Repeat
with remaining bagels.

Crunchy Tuna & Cheese Sandwiches

1 can (9¼ oz.) tuna, drained
   and flaked
⅓ cup sandwich sauce or
   Thousand Island salad
   dressing
⅓ cup mayonnaise or salad
   dressing
¼ cup chopped water chestnuts
1 jar (2 oz.) pimiento-stuffed
   green olives, chopped
1 teaspoon instant minced
   onion
8 or 16 slices whole wheat
   bread, toasted
1 pkg. (5 to 6 oz.) sliced Swiss
   cheese (4 slices, cut in half)

Serves 8

Mix all ingredients except toast
and cheese. Spread on 8 slices
toast. Top each with 1 slice
cheese. Arrange 4 sandwiches
on paper towel-lined plate. Microwave at High 1½ to 2 minutes, or until cheese is softened,
rotating plate ½ turn after half
the time. Repeat with remaining
sandwiches. Cover each with
additional toast slice, if desired.

Hot Hoagies ▲

2 poor boy or Vienna rolls
2 tablespoons prepared
    mustard or salad dressing
8 slices luncheon meat, such
    as bologna or salami
4 slices (¾ oz. each) American
    or Swiss cheese

Serves 4

Cut rolls in half lengthwise.
Spread 1 tablespoon mustard
on bottom half of each roll.
Arrange 4 slices luncheon meat
and 2 slices of cheese on each.
Cover with top half of roll. Wrap
in paper toweling. Place on
plate in oven. Microwave at
High 1 to 2 minutes, or until
cheese melts and rolls are
warm. Top cheese with
shredded lettuce and tomato
and onion slices, if desired.

Fish Sandwiches

1 tablespoon vegetable oil
1 pkg. (7 to 8 oz.) frozen fish
    patties with toasted
    bread crumb coating
4 slices (¾ oz. each) American
    cheese, cut to fit fish patties
4 hamburger buns, split and
    toasted
3 to 4 tablespoons mayonnaise
    or tartar sauce

Serves 4

Preheat 10-in. browning dish at
High 5 minutes. Add oil; tilt dish
to coat. Place fish patties on
dish, pressing each down firmly.
Microwave at High 3 to 4
minutes, or until fish flakes
easily, turning over after half the
time; place cheese slice on
each the last minute. Spread
buns with mayonnaise. Add fish
patties. Garnish with lettuce
leaves, if desired.

Hot Chicken Sandwiches

pictured on page 21

1 can (4½ oz.) chicken spread
2 tablespoons mayonnaise or
    salad dressing
2 tablespoons sweet pickle
    relish, well drained
½ cup shredded Cheddar
    cheese
¼ teaspoon onion powder
6 English muffin halves, toasted

Serves 3

Mix all ingredients except
English muffins in medium bowl.
Spread on toasted muffins.
Arrange in paper towel-lined
12 × 8-in. baking dish.
Microwave at High 1 to 3
minutes, or until cheese melts,
rotating dish after half the time.

Variation:
Hot Ham Sandwich:
Substitute 1 can (4½ oz.) ham
spread for the chicken spread.

Taco Dogs

8 hot dogs
8 hot dog buns

Topping:

1 can (7½ to 10 oz.) beef taco
    filling
1 cup shredded Cheddar
    cheese
1 cup crushed taco chips

Serves 4 to 6

Place 4 hot dogs in buns.
Arrange in 12 × 8-in. baking
dish. Spoon one half of taco
filling over hot dogs. Sprinkle
with half of the cheese and
chips. Cover with wax paper.

Microwave at High 2 to 3
minutes, or until cheese is
melted and buns are hot to the
touch, rotating after half the
cooking time.

Sprinkle with shredded lettuce
and chopped tomato, if desired.
Repeat with remaining hot dogs.

Variations:

Chili Cheese Dogs: Top hot
dogs with 1 can (15 oz.) chili
with beans and 4 slices (¾ oz.
each) American cheese, cut
in half.

Kraut Dogs: Top hot dogs with
mixture of 1 cup drained
sauerkraut and ¼ cup sweet
pickle relish.

Bacon & Cheese Dogs: Use ½
cup processed cheese spread
and 1 tablespoon plus 1
teaspoon bacon bits. Top each
hot dog with 1 tablespoon
cheese spread and about ½
teaspoon bacon bits.

Main Dishes

This section presents 28 easy and delicious recipes to vary convenience meals without sacrificing the convenience. Create these recipes with canned meats and seafood, deli meats, take-out chicken, and frozen entrées.

◄ Chunky Beef Stew & Biscuits

1 pkg. (32 oz.) frozen beef stew
½ pkg. (20 oz.) frozen vegetables for stew
1 jar (12 oz.) brown gravy
2 tablespoons red wine, optional
2 tablespoons butter or margarine
¼ cup seasoned bread crumbs
½ teaspoon paprika, optional
1 pkg. (7½ oz.) buttermilk biscuits, 10-count

Serves 6

Place frozen stew in 12 × 8-in. baking dish or 3-qt. casserole. Cover with plastic wrap. Microwave at High 9 to 10 minutes, stirring to break apart after half the time. Mix in vegetables, gravy and wine; cover. Microwave at High 8 to 10 minutes, or until vegtables are tender, stirring twice.

Place butter in small bowl. Microwave at High 30 to 60 seconds, or until melted. Set aside. Mix bread crumbs and paprika. Dip tops of biscuits in butter, then in crumb mixture. Arrange coated side up on top of stew around edge. Microwave at High 3 to 4 minutes, or until biscuits spring back when touched lightly, rotating ½ turn after half the time.

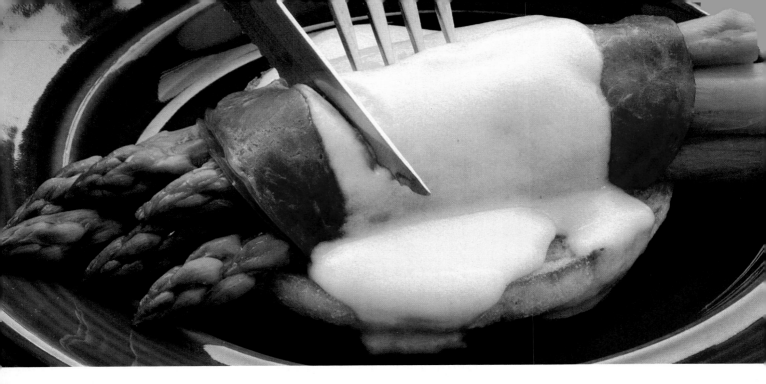

◄ Hamburger Stroganoff

1 lb. ground beef
1 tablespoon instant minced onion
1 can (10¾ oz.) condensed cream of mushroom soup
¾ cup milk
1 can (4 oz.) mushroom stems and pieces, drained
1 teaspoon Worcestershire sauce
½ teaspoon garlic salt
¼ teaspoon pepper
1 cup dairy sour cream

Serves 4 to 6

Crumble ground beef into 2-qt. casserole. Add minced onion. Microwave at High 4 to 5 minutes, or until meat is no longer pink, stirring to break apart after half the time. Drain; break up meat.

Stir in soup, milk, mushrooms, Worcestershire sauce, garlic salt and pepper; cover. Microwave at High 5 to 6 minutes, or until hot and bubbly, stirring after half the time. Blend in sour cream; cover. Microwave at High 1 minute, or until heated. Serve over rice or noodles, if desired.

Asparagus Roll-Ups ▲

1 envelope (1 oz.) hollandaise sauce mix
1 pkg. (10 oz.) frozen asparagus spears
2 tablespoons water
1 pkg. (2½ oz.) sliced dried beef
2 English muffins, halved and toasted

Serves 4

Prepare sauce mix as directed, page 120. Place asparagus spears and water in 1-qt. casserole; cover. Microwave at High 4 to 6 minutes, or until heated, breaking apart after half the time. Drain.

Divide beef into 4 equal portions. Place 5 or 6 asparagus spears on each. Roll up. Place toasted muffin halves in 8 × 8-in. baking dish. Top each with a roll-up. Pour hollandaise sauce evenly over roll-ups. Cover with wax paper. Microwave at 50% (Medium) 2 to 4 minutes, or until heated, rotating dish ½ turn after half the time.

Beef Enchiladas

½ lb. ground beef
2 tablespoons frozen chopped onion or 1½ teaspoons instant minced onion
½ teaspoon salt
2 cups shredded Cheddar cheese, divided
1 can (10 oz.) mild enchilada sauce, divided
1 tablespoon chopped green chilies, optional
6 corn tortillas, 7-in. diameter

Serves 4 to 6

How to Microwave Beef Enchiladas

Crumble ground beef into 1-qt. casserole. Add onion and salt. Microwave at High 2 to 3 minutes, or until meat is no longer pink, stirring after half the cooking time.

Drain. Break apart meat. Stir in 1 cup of the cheese, ¼ cup of the sauce and the chilies. Set aside.

Soften tortillas by placing between paper towels; microwave at High 30 to 45 seconds, or until hot to the touch. Spoon ½ cup meat filling down center of each tortilla. Roll up.

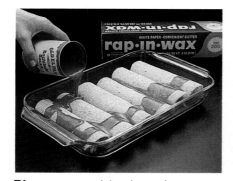

Place seam side down in 12 × 8-in. baking dish. Pour remaining sauce over filled tortillas. Cover with wax paper.

Microwave at High 5 to 6 minutes, or until heated, rotating dish ½ turn after half the time. Top with remaining cheese.

Microwave, uncovered, at High 1½ minutes, or until cheese melts. Garnish with shredded lettuce and sour cream.

◄ Spaghetti Sauce

½ lb. ground beef or bulk
    Italian sausage
1 jar (15 oz.) spaghetti sauce
1 can (4 oz.) mushroom stems
    and pieces, drained
¼ cup sliced pimiento-stuffed
    green olives, optional
1 tablespoon red wine, optional
2 teaspoons sugar
1 teaspoon dried parsley flakes

Makes 2½ cups

Crumble ground beef or sausage into 1½- to 2-qt. casserole. Microwave at High 2 to 4 minutes, or until meat is no longer pink, stirring to break apart after half the time. Drain; break up meat. Stir in remaining ingredients; cover. Microwave at High 3 to 5 minutes, or until hot and bubbly, stirring after half the time. Serve over cooked spaghetti. Sprinkle with Parmesan cheese.

German Potato Salad & Bologna

2 cans (15½ oz. each) German
    potato salad
1 lb. beef ring bologna
1 cup shredded Monterey Jack
    cheese
1 tablespoon dried parsley
    flakes or ½ teaspoon
    caraway seed

Serves 4 to 6

Spread potato salad in 12 × 8-in. baking dish. Remove skin from bologna; cut into ½-in. pieces. Arrange on top of potatoes. Cover with wax paper. Microwave at High 8 to 10 minutes, or until heated, rotating dish every 3 minutes.

Sprinkle with cheese and parsley flakes. Microwave, uncovered, at High 1 to 2 minutes, or until cheese melts.

Ham & Broccoli Rolls ▲

1 envelope (1¼ oz.)
  hollandaise sauce mix
1 pkg. (10 oz.) frozen broccoli
  spears
1 pkg. (8 oz.) boiled ham slices
1 pkg. (8 oz.) sliced Swiss
  cheese, cut to size of
  ham slices

Serves 4

Prepare hollandaise sauce mix
as directed, page 120. Set
aside. Remove outer wrap from
broccoli box; place box in oven.
Microwave at High 3 to 5
minutes, or until defrosted.

Assemble rolls by layering 2
ham slices, 1 cheese slice and
2 broccoli spears. Roll up.
Place seam side down in
12 × 8-in. baking dish. Cover
dish with wax paper. Microwave
at High 4 to 6 minutes, or until
cheese is melted, rotating dish
½ turn after half the time.

Pour sauce evenly over rolls.
Reduce power to 50% (Medium). Microwave 2 to 5 minutes,
or until sauce is heated.

Apricot-Glazed Ham ►

1 can (3 lbs.) ham

Glaze:
1 jar (10 oz.) apricot
  preserves
2 tablespoons packed brown
  sugar
1 teaspoon prepared mustard
¼ teaspoon ground allspice,
  optional

Serves 10 to 12

In 2-cup measure, mix preserves, brown sugar, mustard
and allspice. Microwave at High
1½ to 2 minutes, or until
preserves melt, stirring after half
the cooking time.

Place ham on microwave
roasting rack. Cover with plastic
wrap. Reduce power to 50%
(Medium). Microwave 18 to 24
minutes, or until internal
temperature reaches 130°,
turning ham over and brushing
with glaze after half the time.
Let stand, tented with foil, 5
to 10 minutes. Serve with
remaining glaze.

Variation:
**Cinnamon & Raisin-Glazed
Ham:** Substitute 1 jar (10 oz.)
currant jelly, ½ cup raisins and
¼ teaspoon ground cinnamon
for the glaze ingredients.

◄ Turkey Birds

1 pkg. (6½ oz.) stuffing mix
    with rice
8 slices delicatessen-style
    turkey breast, ¼-in.
1 jar (12 oz.) turkey gravy

Serves 4 to 6

Prepare stuffing mix as
directed, page 131. Divide into
eighths and place on turkey
slices. Roll up. Place roll-ups
seam side down in 12 × 8-in.
baking dish. Pour gravy over
rolls. Cover with wax paper.
Microwave at High 6 to 8
minutes, or until heated, rotating
dish ½ turn after half the time.
Let stand 5 minutes.

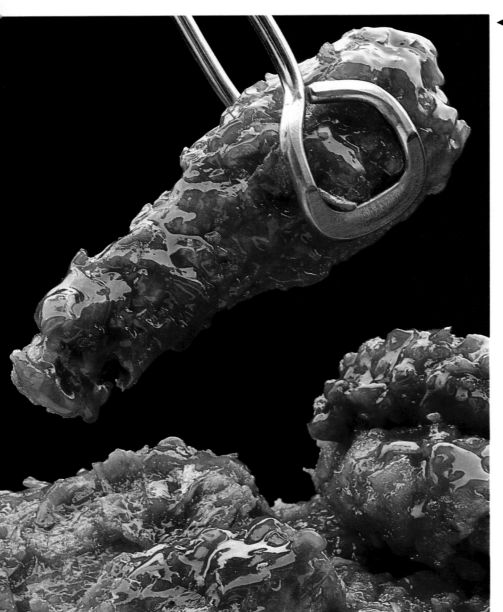

◄ Saucy Fried Chicken

1 cup bottled barbecue sauce
1 cup orange marmalade
1 envelope (single-serving size)
    instant onion soup mix
1 pkg. (2 lbs.) frozen fully-
    cooked fried chicken

Serves 4 to 6

In 4-cup measure or medium
bowl mix barbecue sauce,
marmalade and soup mix.
Microwave at High 3 to 5
minutes, or until heated and
onion is tender.

Prepare frozen chicken as
directed, page 90, brushing
with half of sauce mixture after
half the cooking time. Serve with
remaining sauce.

Variations:
Saucy Deli Chicken: Substitute
9 to 11 pieces delicatessen-
style or take-out fried chicken
for the frozen. Reheat as
directed, page 152, brushing
with half of sauce mixture after
half the reheating time.

Sweet & Sour Chicken:
Substitute Sweet & Sour Sauce,
page 62, for sauce ingredients.

Cranberry-Orange ▲ Turkey Roast

1 can (8 oz.) whole-berry
    cranberry sauce
2 tablespoons orange
    marmalade
1 pkg. (2 lbs.) frozen turkey
    roast

Serves 4 to 6

Place cranberry sauce and marmalade in medium bowl or 2-cup measure. Microwave at High 1½ to 2½ minutes, or until softened, stirring after half the time. Prepare turkey roast as directed, page 90, basting with half of sauce mixture after half the cooking time. Serve with remaining sauce.

Chicken & Rice

1 tablespoon butter or
    margarine
1 can (10¾ oz.) condensed
    cream of mushroom soup
1 can (10¾ oz.) condensed
    cream of celery soup
½ cup milk
2¼ cups instant rice
9 to 11 assorted pieces
    delicatessen-style or
    take-out fried chicken

Serves 4 to 6

Place butter in 12 × 8-in. baking dish. Microwave at High 30 to 45 seconds, or until melted. Blend in soups and milk. Stir in rice. Cover with plastic wrap. Microwave at High 6 to 8 minutes, or until rice is tender.

Arrange chicken skin side up with meatiest portions towards outside of dish. Microwave, uncovered, at High 6 to 8 minutes, or until heated, rearranging pieces after half the time. If chicken was refrigerated, increase time to 8 to 13 minutes.

◄ Salmon Loaf

1 tablespoon bread crumbs
¼ teaspoon paprika
1 cup frozen green peas
1 can (16 oz.) red salmon, drained and cleaned
1 can (4 oz.) sliced mushrooms
½ cup instant rice
2 eggs, slightly beaten
2 teaspoons instant minced onion
1 teaspoon dried parsley flakes
½ teaspoon salt
¼ teaspoon pepper

Serves 4 to 6

Mix bread crumbs and paprika. Grease 8 × 5-in. loaf dish; coat with crumb mixture. Place peas in 2-cup measure. Microwave at High 1 to 2 minutes, or until defrosted. Set aside.

In medium bowl mix salmon, mushrooms with liquid, rice, eggs, onion, parsley, salt and pepper. Gently stir in peas. Press into loaf dish. Microwave at 50% (Medium) 12 to 18 minutes, or until center is firm, rotating once or twice during cooking. Let stand 5 minutes. Loosen edges and invert onto serving plate.

Tuna Hawaiian ▲

2 pkgs. (10 oz. each) frozen Hawaiian-style vegetables
1 can (8 oz.) chunk pineapple, drained and juice reserved
1 tablespoon packed brown sugar
1 tablespoon soy sauce
2 cans (6½ oz. each) tuna, drained
1 can (3 oz.) chow mein noodles
4 servings hot cooked instant rice, page 133

Serves 4

Place contents of vegetable pouches or packages in 8 × 8-in. baking dish. Add pineapple chunks. In 2-cup measure or small bowl combine reserved pineapple juice, brown sugar and soy sauce. Pour over vegetable mixture. Cover with plastic wrap. Microwave at High 6 to 8 minutes, or until heated, stirring after half the time. Stir in tuna. Microwave at High 1½ to 2½ minutes, or until heated. Stir in chow mein noodles. Serve over rice.

Variation:
Substitute 2 cans (5 to 6¾ oz. each) chunked chicken or ham, flaked, for the tuna.

Creamed Salmon ▶

1 pkg. (8 oz.) frozen peas in
    cream sauce
1 cup milk
1 tablespoon butter or
    margarine
1 can (7¾ oz.) salmon, drained
    and cleaned
1 can (4 oz.) mushroom stems
    and pieces, drained

Serves 4

Place contents of pea package
in 1½-qt. casserole. Add milk
and butter; cover. Microwave at
High 5 to 6 minutes, or until
sauce is thickened, stirring after
half the cooking time.

Stir in salmon and mushrooms;
cover. Microwave at High 1 to 2
minutes, or until heated, stirring
after half the cooking time.
Serve over toast points or patty
shells, if desired.

Shrimp Newburg

¼ cup butter or margarine
2 tablespoons all-purpose flour
½ teaspoon salt
¼ teaspoon paprika
1 can (13 oz.) evaporated milk
2 egg yolks, slightly beaten
2 cans (4 oz. each) tiny
    shrimp, rinsed and drained
¼ cup sherry
1 pkg. (10 oz.) frozen patty
    shells, prepared
    conventionally

Serves 4 to 6

Place butter in 2-qt. casserole
or large bowl. Microwave at
High 30 to 60 seconds, or until
melted. Blend in flour, salt and
paprika. Stir in milk. Microwave
at High 3 to 5 minutes, or until
thickened, stirring after 2 minutes and then every minute.

Stir small amount of hot mixture
into egg yolks; return to hot mixture. Stir in shrimp. Microwave
at High 1 to 2 minutes, or until
heated. Stir in sherry. Serve
over patty shells.

Crunchy Taco Bake ▲

1 lb. ground beef
½ cup frozen chopped onions or 2 tablespoons dried onion flakes
1 can (15 oz.) hot chili with beans
1 can (15 oz.) tomato sauce
1 can (6 oz.) tomato paste
1½ teaspoons chili powder
½ teaspoon salt
2 cups coarsely crushed corn chips, divided
1 cup shredded Cheddar cheese

Serves 4

Crumble ground beef into 2-qt. casserole or medium bowl. Add onions. Microwave at High 4 to 6 minutes, or until meat is no longer pink, stirring to break apart after half the time. Drain. Stir in chili with beans, tomato sauce, tomato paste, chili powder and salt. Microwave at High 6 to 8 minutes, or until heated and flavors are blended.

Sprinkle 1 cup corn chips in 8 × 8-in. baking dish. Spoon meat mixture over chips. Top with remaining corn chips. Sprinkle with cheese. Microwave at High 1 to 2 minutes, or until cheese melts.

Cantonese Ham Casserole

1 envelope (1¼ oz.) sour cream sauce mix
1 pkg. (9 oz.) frozen French-style green beans
2 cans (5 to 6¾ oz. each) chunked ham, drained or 2 cups cubed fully cooked ham
1 can (8 oz.) sliced water chestnuts, drained
¼ cup dairy sour cream
2 tablespoons soy sauce
1 can (3 oz.) French fried onion rings, divided

Serves 4

Prepare sour cream sauce mix as directed on package. Set aside. Place green beans in 1½-qt. casserole; cover. Microwave at High 4 to 6 minutes, or until heated, stirring to break apart after half the time. Stir in sour cream sauce, ham, water chestnuts, sour cream and soy sauce.

Reduce power to 50% (Medium). Microwave 8 to 12 minutes, or until heated, stirring 3 or 4 times during cooking. Stir in half of the onion rings. Top with remaining onion rings. Microwave at 50% (Medium) 2 to 4 minutes, or until onion rings are heated, rotating once.

Calico Beans ►

6 slices bacon, cut into ½-in. pieces
½ cup frozen chopped onion or 2 tablespoons dried onion flakes
2 cans (16 oz. each) baked beans
1 can (16 oz.) lima beans, drained
1 can (15½ oz.) garbanzo beans, drained
3 cups cubed ham, ½-in. pieces
⅔ cup barbecue sauce
½ cup packed brown sugar
1 tablespoon prepared mustard
1½ teaspoons Worcestershire sauce
½ teaspoon salt

Serves 6 to 8

Place bacon in 3-qt. casserole; cover with paper towel. Microwave at High 4 to 5 minutes, or until crisp. Drain fat, reserving 2 tablespoons in casserole. Drain bacon on paper towel.

Add onion to fat in casserole. Microwave, uncovered, at High 1½ to 2 minutes, or until tender. Stir in bacon and remaining ingredients; cover. Microwave at High 14 to 16 minutes, or until heated, stirring 2 or 3 times during cooking.

Turkey Divan Casserole ▲

2 pkgs. (8 oz. each) frozen
  chopped broccoli
1 can (10¾ oz.) condensed
  cream of chicken soup
½ cup mayonnaise or salad
  dressing
½ cup milk

¼ teaspoon salt
1 lb. thinly sliced, fully cooked
  turkey breast
1 can (1½ oz.) shoestring
  potatoes, divided
6 slices (¾ oz. each)
  pasteurized process
  American cheese

Serves 4 to 6

Remove outer wrap from broccoli packages; place in oven.
Microwave at High 5 to 6 minutes, or until defrosted. Drain.

Mix soup, mayonnaise, milk and salt. Spread half in 12 × 8-in.
baking dish. Arrange broccoli in dish. Top with turkey and half the
shoestring potatoes. Pour remaining soup mixture over top. Cover
with wax paper.

Microwave at High 8 to 11 minutes, or until heated, rotating dish ½
turn after half the time. Arrange cheese slices on top; sprinkle with
remaining shoestring potatoes. Microwave, uncovered, at High 3 to
4 minutes, or until cheese melts, rotating dish ½ turn after half the
cooking time.

Turkey Oriental

2 cups cubed, cooked turkey or
  chicken, ½-in. pieces
2 cups instant rice
1 pkg. (10 oz.) frozen stir-fry
  vegetables with seasonings
1 cup water
3 tablespoons soy sauce
1 tablespoon chopped pimiento
1 teaspoon instant chicken
  bouillon granules

Serves 4

Combine all ingredients in 2-qt.
casserole; cover. Microwave at
High 12 to 14 minutes, or until
rice is tender and liquid is
absorbed, stirring after half the
cooking time. Stir; let stand,
covered, 3 minutes.

NOTE: 2 cans (5 to 6¾ oz.
each) chunked chicken or
turkey can be substituted for the
cooked turkey or chicken.

Wild Rice Casserole ▲

1 pkg. (6 oz.) long grain and
   wild rice mix
1 pkg. (10 oz.) frozen chopped
   spinach
2 cups cubed, cooked turkey
   or chicken, ½-in. pieces,
   drained
½ cup dairy sour cream

Serves 4 to 6

Prepare rice as directed for 20
to 30 Minute Rice, page 133.
Let stand as directed in chart.

Place spinach in 1-qt. casserole; cover. Microwave at High
4 to 6 minutes, or until heated
and tender, stirring after half the
time to break apart. Drain well.

Stir chicken and spinach into
rice; cover. Microwave at High
2 to 4 minutes, or until heated.
Stir in sour cream. Let stand,
covered, 3 minutes.

NOTE: 2 cans (5 to 6¾ oz.
each) chunked chicken or
turkey, drained, can be
substituted for the cooked
turkey or chicken.

Chicken Romanoff ►

1 pkg. (10 oz.) frozen chopped
   spinach
1 pkg. (5½ oz.) noodles
   romanoff mix
2 cans (5 to 6¾ oz. each)
   chunked chicken, drained
   and flaked
1 cup shredded Swiss cheese
¼ teaspoon poultry seasoning
2 tablespoons grated
   Parmesan cheese
¼ cup sliced almonds

Serves 4

Remove outer wrap from spinach package; place in oven.
Microwave at High 4 minutes, or
until defrosted. Drain. Prepare
noodles romanoff mix as
directed, page 131. Add
spinach, chicken, Swiss cheese
and poultry seasoning. Press
mixture into 8 × 8-in. baking
dish. Sprinkle with Parmesan
cheese. Reduce power to 50%
(Medium). Microwave 10 to 15
minutes, or until heated, rotating
¼ turn 3 or 4 times during
cooking. Sprinkle with almonds.

Tuna & Potato Chip ▲ Casserole

3 cups crushed potato chips
1 can (10¾ oz.) condensed
     cream of mushroom soup
1 can (6½ oz.) tuna, drained
1 can (4 oz.) mushroom stems
     and pieces, drained
1 jar (2 oz.) pimiento-stuffed
     green olives, sliced
½ cup shredded Cheddar
     cheese
½ cup milk
2 tablespoons frozen chopped
     onion or 1½ teaspoons
     dried onion flakes

Serves 4

Place one-third of crushed chips in 1½-qt. casserole. In medium bowl combine remaining ingredients except chips. Spread half of tuna mixture over chips. Top with another one-third of chips and remaining tuna. Sprinkle remaining chips over top. Microwave at High 4 to 6 minutes, or until heated, rotating dish ¼ turn after half the cooking time.

Tuna Potato Casserole

1 pkg. (9 oz.) frozen French-
     style green beans
1 pkg. (5½ oz.) au gratin
     potato mix
2½ cups hot water
1 can (6½ oz.) tuna, drained
¾ cup milk
1 envelope (single-serving
     size) instant onion soup
     mix
2 tablespoons butter or
     margarine
1 can (3 oz.) French fried
     onion rings

Serves 4 to 6

Place green beans in 2-qt. casserole; cover. Microwave at High 3 to 4 minutes, or until beans can be broken apart easily. Mix in remaining ingredients except onion rings; cover. Microwave at High 18 to 25 minutes, or until potatoes are tender and sauce thickened, stirring 3 or 4 times during cooking. Sprinkle with onion rings during last 2 minutes of cooking. Let stand 5 minutes.

Fried Rice

1 pkg. (6¼ oz.) fried rice mix
2 tablespoons butter or
     margarine
2 cups hot water
1 pkg. (10 oz.) frozen large
     cooked shrimp
1 pkg. (6 oz.) frozen pea
     pods
2 eggs
1½ teaspoons soy sauce
1 can (8 oz.) sliced water
     chestnuts, drained

Serves 4

Place rice and butter in 2-qt. casserole. Microwave at High 2 to 3 minutes, or until rice begins to brown, stirring after half the time. Stir in hot water and seasoning mix from rice package; cover. Microwave at High 5 to 7 minutes, or until boiling. Stir. Reduce power to 50% (Medium). Microwave 10 to 20 minutes, or until rice is tender. Let stand, covered, 10 to 15 minutes, or until no visible moisture remains in bottom of dish.

Place shrimp in single layer in 8 × 8-in. baking dish. Microwave at 50% (Medium) 2 to 4 minutes, or until no longer icy, stirring after half the time. Rinse under cool water. Set aside.

Place pea pods in 1-qt. casserole. Increase power to High. Microwave 2 to 4 minutes, or until defrosted. Set aside.

Beat eggs and soy sauce in medium bowl. Increase power to High. Microwave 1½ to 2 minutes, or until eggs are al- most set, stirring after half the cooking time. Break up eggs into small pieces.

Stir eggs, water chestnuts, shrimp and pea pods into rice. Microwave at High 1 to 2 minutes, or until heated.

Shrimp & Rice Medley ▲

1 pkg. (10 oz.) frozen large
   cooked shrimp
2 tablespoons butter or
   margarine
⅓ cup seasoned bread crumbs
1 pkg. (10 oz.) frozen rice with
   peas and mushrooms

1 pkg. (10 oz.) frozen long
   grain white and wild rice
1 can (10¾ oz.) condensed
   cream of shrimp soup
2 tablespoons white wine

Serves 4

Place shrimp in single layer in 8 × 8-in. baking dish. Microwave at 50% (Medium) 2 to 4 minutes, or until no longer icy, stirring to break apart after half the time. Rinse under cool water. Set aside.

Place butter in small bowl or custard cup. Increase power to High. Microwave 30 to 60 seconds, or until melted. Stir in bread crumbs. Set aside.

Cut a large "X" in one side of each rice pouch. Place pouches side by side, cut side down, in 12 × 8-in. baking dish. Microwave at High 6 to 8 minutes, or until heated. Empty rice into dish. Stir. Add shrimp, soup and wine. Cover with wax paper. Microwave at High 8 to 9 minutes, or until heated, stirring every 3 minutes. Sprinkle bread crumb mixture over top.

Deli Seafood Casserole

2 tablespoons butter or
   margarine
¼ cup plus 2 tablespoons
   seasoned bread crumbs
1 qt. delicatessen-style
   macaroni tuna salad
2 cans (4¼ oz. each) shrimp,
   drained and rinsed
1 cup frozen peas
¼ cup milk

Serves 4 to 6

Place butter in small dish. Microwave at High 30 to 60 seconds, or until melted. Stir in bread crumbs. Set aside.

Combine remaining ingredients in 2-qt. casserole; cover. Microwave at High 6 to 8 minutes, or until heated, stirring after half the time. Sprinkle with crumbs. Microwave at High 1 to 2 minutes, or until heated.

Eggs & Cheese

Omelets, quiches and other egg dishes acquire greater variety and ease of preparation when you use convenience foods for fillings and flavorings. With packaged sauces and shredded cheese, you can make fondues, rarebits, or a richer-tasting version of popular macaroni and cheese.

Puffy Omelet

1 tablespoon butter or
  margarine
6 eggs, separated
⅓ cup milk
½ teaspoon salt
¼ teaspoon baking powder
⅛ teaspoon pepper

Serves 2 to 4

Place butter in 10-in. pie plate. Microwave at High 30 to 60 seconds, or until melted. Beat egg whites in large bowl until stiff but not dry. Blend egg yolks, milk, salt, baking powder and pepper. Fold into beaten egg whites. Pour into pie plate.

Reduce power to 50% (Medium). Microwave 3 to 5 minutes, or until partially set. Lift edges with spatula so uncooked portion spreads evenly. Microwave 3 to 5 minutes, or until center is almost set. Spoon half of one of the fillings in the following recipes over half of the omelet. Loosen omelet with spatula and fold in half. Gently slide onto serving plate. Spoon remaining filling over top.

Strawberry-Orange Omelet

pictured at left

1 pkg. (10 oz.) frozen
  strawberries
1 teaspoon cornstarch
1 can (8 oz.) mandarin orange
  sections, drained
  Puffy Omelet, left

Serves 2 to 4

Defrost strawberries as directed, page 96. Empty into 1-qt. casserole. Set aside.

Drain strawberry juice into 1-cup measure or small bowl. Blend in cornstarch. Microwave at High 2 to 3 minutes, or until clear and thickened, stirring after each minute. Mix strawberries, oranges and sauce just before serving. Prepare Puffy Omelet; add fruit filling as directed. Sprinkle omelet with powdered sugar, if desired.

Ham & Cheese Omelet

1 envelope (1¼ oz.) cheese
  sauce mix
½ can (6¾ oz.) chunked ham,
  flaked
  Puffy Omelet, left

Serves 2 to 4

Prepare cheese sauce mix as directed, page 120. Stir in ham. Prepare Puffy Omelet; add ham and cheese filling as directed.

Variation:
Omit ham. Add cheese sauce as directed. Sprinkle with 2 tablespoons bacon bits or 1 can (3 oz.) French fried onion rings.

Mushroom Omelet

1 can (7½ oz.) semi-
  condensed cream of
  mushroom soup
½ cup milk
1 can (3 to 4 oz.) mushroom
  stems and pieces, drained
  Puffy Omelet, left

Serves 2 to 4

In small bowl, blend soup and milk. Microwave at High 3 to 4 minutes, or until heated. Stir in mushrooms. Prepare Puffy Omelet; add mushroom filling as directed.

◄ Curried Egg Foo Yung

1 pkg. (30¼ oz.) stir-fry egg
  foo yung dinner mix
1¼ cups cold water
2 tablespoons packed brown
  sugar
2 tablespoons dry white wine
4 eggs
2 tablespoons sunflower nuts,
  optional
1 tablespoon soy sauce
¼ to ½ teaspoon curry powder

Serves 4

In small bowl mix sauce mix,
cold water, brown sugar and
wine. Microwave at High 5 to 6
minutes, or until clear and
thickened, stirring after 2
minutes and then every minute.

In medium bowl beat eggs. Stir
in seasoning mix, drained and
rinsed vegetables, nuts, soy
sauce and curry powder. Microwave at High 3 to 6 minutes, or
until slightly set, stirring twice.

Preheat browning dish at High 5
minutes. Ladle four patties of
mixture onto dish. Microwave at
High 2 minutes; turn. Microwave
2 to 3 minutes longer, or until
patties are set and light brown.
Reheat sauce at High 1 to 2
minutes. Serve over patties.

Spinach Quiche ▲

1 frozen unbaked 9-in.
  pie shell
1 pkg. (12 oz.) frozen spinach
  soufflé
2 eggs, slightly beaten
¼ cup milk
1 tablespoon bacon bits,
  optional
½ cup shredded Cheddar
  cheese, divided

Serves 6

Microwave pastry shell as
directed, page 101. Remove
frozen soufflé from foil tray.
Place in medium mixing bowl.
Microwave at 50% (Medium) 4
to 5 minutes, or until defrosted,
breaking apart after half the
cooking time. Stir in eggs, milk
and bacon bits.

Microwave at 50% (Medium) 5
to 6 minutes, or until slightly
thickened, stirring every 2
minutes. Stir in ¼ cup of the
cheese. Pour into pastry shell.
Place in oven on inverted
saucer. Microwave at 50%
(Medium) 7 to 15 minutes, or
until set, rotating every 2
minutes. Sprinkle with remaining
¼ cup cheese during last 1 to 2
minutes of cooking time.

Bacon & Egg Sandwiches ▲

4 teaspoons butter or margarine
4 eggs
1 pkg. (6 oz.) ready-to-eat
   Canadian bacon slices or
   8 slices bacon, microwaved
   as directed, page 149

4 slices (¾ oz. each) American
   cheese
4 English muffins, split and
   toasted

Serves 4

Place 1 teaspoon butter in each of four 6-oz. custard cups. Microwave all at High 30 to 60 seconds, or until melted. Place 1 egg in each cup; scramble with fork. Arrange cups in circle in oven. Microwave at High 40 to 60 seconds, or until set but slightly moist, stirring eggs and rearranging cups once. Let stand 2 minutes.

Assemble sandwich by layering 1 slice cheese, 1 scrambled egg and 1 Canadian bacon slice or 2 bacon slices between each split muffin. Wrap each sandwich in paper towel. Place in circle in oven. Microwave at 50% (Medium) 2 to 2½ minutes, or until cheese is melted and sandwiches are warm to the touch, rearranging after half the time.

Double Cheese Macaroni & Cheese

1 pkg. (7¼ oz.) macaroni and
   cheese dinner mix
1 cup shredded Cheddar
   cheese
½ cup dairy sour cream
2 teaspoons dried chives
   Dash red pepper

Serves 4

Prepare dinner mix according to directions, page 128. Blend in remaining ingredients. Microwave at 50% (Medium) 3 to 5 minutes, or until heated, stirring after half the time.

Variation:
Substitute 1 qt. delicatessen-prepared macaroni and cheese for the dinner mix.

Burrito Pie

1 pkg. (3 oz.) cream cheese
1 can (17 oz.) refried beans
1 egg, slightly beaten
2 tablespoons chopped green
  chilies
4 flour tortillas, 9-in. diameter
3 cups shredded Cheddar
  cheese

Serves 6

Place cream cheese in medium bowl. Microwave at 50% (Medium) 30 to 60 seconds, or until softened. Mix in beans, egg and green chilies.

In 9-in. round cake dish layer 1 tortilla, scant ⅔ cup bean mixture and about ¾ cup Cheddar cheese. Repeat 3 times ending with cheese. Microwave at 50% (Medium) 10 to 15 minutes, or until heated, rotating every 3 minutes.

Cheese Puff

1 envelope (1¼ oz.) cheese
  sauce mix
1 teaspoon dried parsley flakes
½ teaspoon dry mustard
6 eggs, separated

Serves 4

Prepare cheese sauce mix as directed, page 120, adding parsley flakes and mustard before microwaving.

Beat egg yolks in medium bowl until thick and lemon colored. In large bowl beat egg whites until stiff but not dry. Gradually stir egg yolks into cheese mixture. Fold into egg whites.

Pour into 2-qt. casserole. Microwave at 30% (Medium-Low) 12 to 15 minutes, or until top is dry, rotating dish 3 or 4 times.

Broccoli & Cheese Strata ▲

1 pkg. (10 oz.) frozen chopped
  broccoli
6 slices whole wheat bread, cut
  into ½-in. cubes
1 cup milk
1 cup shredded Cheddar
  cheese
4 eggs, slightly beaten
1 teaspoon salt

Serves 4 to 6

Place broccoli in 1- to 1½-qt. casserole; cover. Microwave at High 5 to 6 minutes, or until heated, stirring after half the time. Drain thoroughly. In medium bowl combine bread cubes, milk, cheese, eggs and salt. Stir in broccoli. Spread mixture evenly in 8 × 8-in. baking dish. Cover. Refrigerate 4 hours or overnight.

Cover with wax paper. Place on inverted saucer in oven. Microwave at High 3 minutes. Rotate ¼ turn. Reduce power to 50% (Medium). Microwave 15 to 25 minutes, or until set, rotating 3 or 4 times during cooking and removing wax paper after half the time. Let stand 5 minutes.

Swiss Cheese Fondue ▶

4 cups shredded Swiss cheese
3 tablespoons all-purpose flour
⅛ teaspoon garlic powder
1 cup dry white wine
   Dash ground nutmeg
   Cubes of French bread

Serves 4

Shake cheese, flour and garlic powder together in plastic bag. Measure wine into medium bowl. Microwave at 50% (Medium) 2 to 3 minutes, or until wine is hot but not boiling. Stir in cheese mixture. Microwave at 50% (Medium) 6 to 8 minutes, or until smooth, stirring vigorously with wire whip every 2 minutes. Sprinkle with nutmeg. Serve hot with bread cubes for dipping.

Cheese & Mushroom Rarebit

1 envelope (1 oz.)
   white sauce mix
¼ cup sherry
½ teaspoon dry mustard
2 cups shredded Cheddar
   cheese
1 can (3 to 4 oz.) mushroom,
   stems and pieces, drained
4 English muffins, split and
   toasted

Serves 4

Prepare sauce mix as directed, page 120. Blend in sherry and mustard. Microwave at High 1 to 2 minutes, or until heated. With wire whip beat in cheese until melted and blended. Reduce power to 50% (Medium). Microwave 2 to 3 minutes to heat, stirring after half the time. Stir in mushrooms. Serve over muffins.

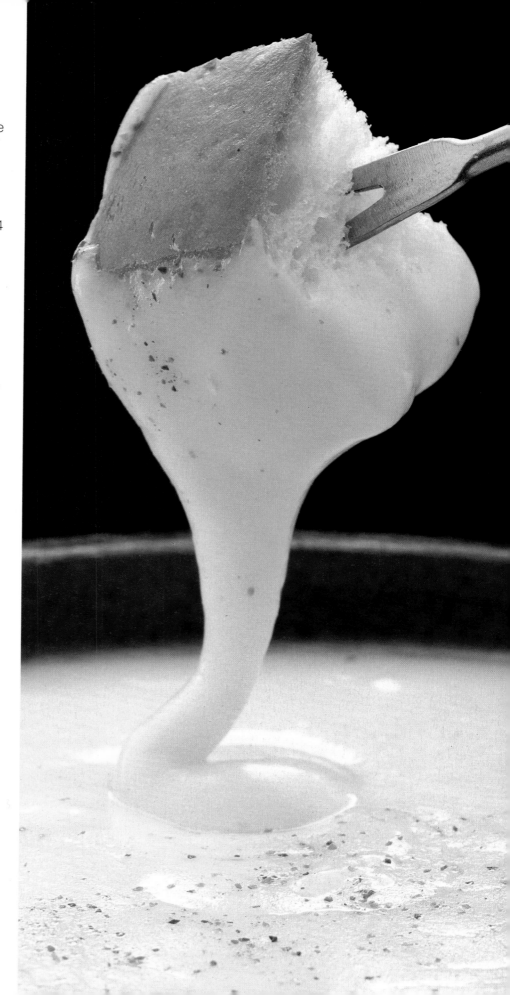

Vegetables

Vegetables are an important part of nutritious meals. Sauces, garnishes and clever combinations can dress up canned or frozen vegetables to give them a starring role in the menu.

◄ Oriental Asparagus & Carrots

1 pkg. (9 oz.) frozen asparagus in butter sauce
1 pkg. (10 oz.) frozen carrots in butter sauce
3 tablespoons bottled sweet and sour sauce
1 tablespoon soy sauce
2 tablespoons sunflower nuts

Serves 4 to 6

Cut a large "X" in one side of each pouch. Place side by side, cut side down, in 2-qt. casserole. Microwave at High 6 to 9 minutes, or until heated. Empty vegetables into casserole; stir. Mix in sweet and sour sauce and soy sauce. Microwave at High 1 to 2 minutes, or until heated. Sprinkle sunflower nuts over vegetables.

◄ Creamy Asparagus

1 pkg. (8 oz.) frozen aspara-
    gus cuts or spears
1 envelope (single-serving
    size) cream of chicken
    soup mix
½ cup hot water
⅛ teaspoon ground marjoram,
    optional

Serves 4

Place asparagus in 1- to 1½-qt.
casserole; cover. Microwave at
High 4 to 6 minutes, or until
tender, stirring after half the
time; set aside.

In 2-cup measure combine
soup mix, water and marjoram.
Microwave at High 1 to 2
minutes, or until thickened,
stirring after every minute. Pour
over asparagus.

Creamy Deviled Lima Beans

2 pkgs. (10 oz. each) frozen
    baby lima beans
1 cup dairy sour cream
1 can (8 oz.) sliced
    mushrooms, drained
1 can (3 oz.) deviled ham
¼ cup frozen chopped onion or
    1 tablespoon dried onion
    flakes
1 teaspoon salt
½ cup shredded Cheddar
    cheese

Serves 4 to 6

Place lima beans in 2-qt. casserole; cover. Microwave at High
6 to 8 minutes, or until heated
and tender, stirring to break
apart after half the time. Drain.

In small bowl mix sour cream,
mushrooms, ham, onion and
salt. Stir into lima beans; cover.
Reduce power to 50%
(Medium). Microwave 2 to 4
minutes, or until heated, stirring
once during cooking. Sprinkle
with cheese. Microwave at 50%
(Medium) 2 to 3 minutes, or
until cheese melts.

Cheesy Green ▲ Beans Almondine

2 pkgs. (9 oz. each) frozen
   French-style green beans
1 can (4 oz.) mushroom stems
   and pieces, drained
1 pkg. (8 oz.) pasteurized
   process cheese loaf,
   cut into ½-in. cubes
¼ cup sliced almonds

Serves 4 to 6

Place green beans in 2-qt.
casserole; cover. Microwave at
High 8 to 10 minutes, or until
tender, stirring to break apart
after half the time. Drain. Stir in
mushrooms and cheese; cover.
Microwave at High 2 to 3
minutes, or until cheese melts,
stirring after half the time.
Sprinkle with almonds.

Baked Beans

6 slices bacon, cut into ½-in.
   pieces
¾ cup frozen chopped onions
   or 3 tablespoons dried
   onion flakes
2 cans (16 oz. each) pork and
   beans
¼ cup packed brown sugar
¼ cup beer
1 tablespoon prepared
   mustard
1 tablespoon bottled
   barbecue sauce
½ teaspoon chili powder
⅛ teaspoon pepper

Serves 4 to 6

Place bacon and onion in 2-qt.
casserole; cover. Microwave at
High 5 to 6 minutes, or until
crisp. Drain all but 2 tablespoons fat. Stir in remaining
ingredients. Microwave at High
7 to 9 minutes, or until heated,
stirring after half the time.

Beets With Cream ▲ Cheese Sauce

1 can (16 oz.) sliced beets,
   drained and 2 table-
   spoons juice reserved
1 pkg. (3 oz.) cream cheese
1 tablespoon white vinegar
1½ teaspoons sugar
⅛ to ¼ teaspoon nutmeg

Serves 4

In 1-qt. casserole combine
beets and reserved juice; cover.
Microwave at High 2½ to 3
minutes, or until heated, stirring
after half the time. Set aside.

Place cream cheese in small
bowl. Microwave at High 15 to
30 seconds, or until softened.
Blend in vinegar and sugar until
smooth. Top each serving of
beets with a spoonful of cream
cheese mixture. Sprinkle
nutmeg over sauce.

◄ Broccoli Onion Bake

2 pkgs. (10 oz. each) frozen
  broccoli spears
1 can (10¾ oz.) condensed
  cream of chicken soup
1 cup shredded Cheddar
  cheese, divided
1 can (3 oz.) French fried
  onion rings, divided
¼ cup milk
½ teaspoon salt
⅛ teaspoon pepper

Serves 4 to 6

Place broccoli in 12 × 8-in.
baking dish. Cover with plastic
wrap. Microwave at High 6 to 9
minutes, or until tender-crisp,
stirring to break apart after half
the time.

Arrange broccoli spears with
heads towards center of dish. In
small bowl blend soup, ½ cup
of the cheese, half of the onion
rings, the milk, salt and pepper.
Pour over broccoli spears;
cover. Microwave at High 3 to 5
minutes, or until heated, rotating
dish ½ turn after half the time.
Sprinkle with remaining cheese,
then onion rings. Microwave at
High 1½ to 3 minutes, or until
cheese melts.

Double Cheese ▲ Broccoli Casserole

2 pkgs. (10 oz. each) frozen
  chopped broccoli
3 eggs, slightly beaten
3 tablespoons all-purpose flour
1 teaspoon salt
¼ teaspoon onion powder
1 cup cream-style cottage
  cheese
1 cup shredded Cheddar
  cheese
1 can (8 oz.) sliced water
  chestnuts, drained

Serves 4 to 6

Remove outer wrap from
broccoli packages; place
packages in oven. Microwave at
High 4 to 6 minutes, or until
defrosted, rearranging after half
the time. Drain well. In medium
bowl blend eggs, flour, salt and
onion powder. Stir in remaining
ingredients and broccoli.

Microwave at High 3 to 6
minutes, or until cheese melts
and mixture begins to set,
stirring after the first 2 minutes
and then after every minute.
Pour into 8 × 8-in. baking dish.
Cover with wax paper. Place in
oven on inverted saucer.
Reduce power to 50%
(Medium). Microwave 15 to 25
minutes, or until set, rotating
dish ¼ turn every 3 minutes.

Crunchy-Topped Brussels Sprouts ▲

1 pkg. (6 oz.) corn bread or
   chicken flavor stuffing mix
2 pkgs. (10 oz. each) or 1 pkg.
   (20 oz.) frozen Brussels
   sprouts
1 cup hot water

2 teaspoons instant chicken
   bouillon granules
¼ cup powdered non-dairy
   creamer
2 tablespoons all-purpose flour
¼ cup chopped pecans

Serves 4 to 6

Prepare stuffing mix as directed, page 131. Set aside. Place
Brussels sprouts in 2-qt. casserole; cover. Microwave at High 6 to
8 minutes, or until tender, stirring to break apart after half the
cooking time. Drain.

Stir bouillon into hot water until dissolved. In medium bowl or 4-cup
measure mix non-dairy creamer and flour. Blend in bouillon mixture
until smooth. Microwave at High 2½ to 3½ minutes, or until
thickened. Pour over Brussels sprouts. Top with prepared stuffing.
Sprinkle with pecans. Microwave at High 2 to 4 minutes, or until
heated, rotating dish ½ turn after half the time.

Sunshine Carrots

1 tablespoon butter or
   margarine
2 tablespoons honey
½ teaspoon lemon juice
1 can (16 oz.) sliced carrots,
   drained

Serves 4

Place butter in 1-qt. casserole.
Microwave at High 30 to 45
seconds, or until melted. Mix in
honey and lemon juice. Stir in
carrots. Microwave at High 2
to 3 minutes, or until heated,
stirring after half the time.

Zesty Tomatoed Carrots

  1 can (10¾ oz.) condensed
    tomato soup
⅔ cup sugar
½ cup bottled oil and vinegar
    salad dressing
¼ cup frozen chopped onion or
    1 tablespoon dried
    onion flakes
¼ cup frozen chopped green
    pepper
  1 teaspoon Worcestershire
    sauce
½ teaspoon salt
  1 pkg. (16 oz.) frozen crinkle-
    cut carrots

Serves 6

In 2-qt. casserole blend all
ingredients except carrots. Stir
in carrots; cover. Microwave at
High 15 to 18 minutes, or until
tender-crisp, stirring after half
the cooking time. Refrigerate 6
to 8 hours or overnight.

Italian Vegetable Combo

  1 pkg. (10 oz.) frozen broccoli
    flowerets
  1 pkg. (10 oz.) frozen
    cauliflowerets
  1 jar (4½ oz.) whole
    mushrooms, drained
½ cup bottled Italian salad
    dressing
  1 medium green pepper, cut
    into 1-in. chunks, optional

Serves 6

Place broccoli and cauliflower in
a 2-qt. casserole. Cover. Microwave at High 6 to 8 minutes, or
until thoroughly heated, stirring
to break apart after half the
cooking time. Add mushrooms,
dressing and green pepper.
Microwave at High 2 to 3 minutes, or until thoroughly heated
and pepper is tender-crisp.

Variation:
Refrigerate after cooking; serve
as an appetizer.

Cheesy Cauliflower ▲

2 tablespoons butter or
  margarine
¾ cup herb-seasoned stuffing
  mix
2 pkgs. (10 oz. each) frozen
  cauliflower
1 envelope (1¼ oz.) white
  sauce mix
½ cup pasteurized process
  cheese spread

          Serves 4 to 6

Place butter in medium bowl.
Microwave at High 30 to 45
seconds, or until melted. Add
stuffing; toss to coat. Set aside.

Place cauliflower in 2-qt. casserole; cover. Microwave at High
8 to 10 minutes, or until heated,
stirring after half the time to
break apart. Drain; set aside.

Prepare white sauce mix as
directed, page 120. Add
cheese, stirring constantly until
melted; pour over cauliflower.
Top with stuffing mixture.
Microwave at High 3 to 4
minutes, or until heated, rotating
¼ turn after half the time.

Mexicali Corn Casserole ▶

¼ cup butter or margarine
1 pkg. (8½ oz.) corn bread mix
1 can (8 oz.) cream-style corn
1 can (8 oz.) whole kernel
  corn, drained
1 cup dairy sour cream
½ cup shredded Cheddar
  cheese
3 eggs, slightly beaten
2 tablespoons chopped green
  chilies
½ teaspoon salt
⅛ teaspoon paprika

          Serves 4 to 6

Place butter in 3-qt. casserole.
Microwave at High 30 to 60
seconds, or until melted. Blend
in remaining ingredients except
paprika. Microwave at High 2 to
4 minutes, or until cheese melts
and mixture begins to set, stirring 2 or 3 times during cooking.

Pour into 8 × 8-in. baking dish.
Cover with wax paper. Reduce
power to 50% (Medium). Microwave 12 to 18 minutes, or until
set, rotating dish ¼ turn every 3
minutes. Sprinkle with paprika.

◄ Hawaiian Pea Pods & Carrots

1 can (8½ oz.) pineapple
   chunks, drained and 2
   tablespoons juice reserved
2 tablespoons soy sauce
1 tablespoon honey
1½ teaspoons cornstarch
1 pkg. (16 oz.) frozen baby
   carrots
1 pkg. (6 oz.) frozen Chinese
   pea pods

Serves 4

In small bowl or 2-cup measure mix reserved pineapple juice, soy sauce, honey and cornstarch. Microwave at High 1 to 1½ minutes, or until clear and thickened, stirring after half the time. Set aside. Place carrots in 2-qt. casserole; cover. Microwave at High 8 to 10 minutes, or until tender-crisp, stirring after half the time.

Cut pineapple chunks in half. Add pineapple and pea pods to carrots; cover. Microwave at High 2 to 4 minutes, or until tender, stirring after half the time to break apart pea pods. Drain. Add sauce, tossing to coat. Microwave at High 1 to 2 minutes, or until heated.

Italian Peas

1 pkg. (10 oz.) frozen tiny
   green peas
¼ cup bottled creamy Italian
   salad dressing
¼ cup dairy sour cream
½ teaspoon sugar
¼ teaspoon celery seed

Serves 4

Place peas in 1-qt. casserole; cover. Microwave at High 4 to 6 minutes, or until tender, stirring after half the time to break apart. Mix in remaining ingredients; cover. Microwave at High 1 minute, or until heated.

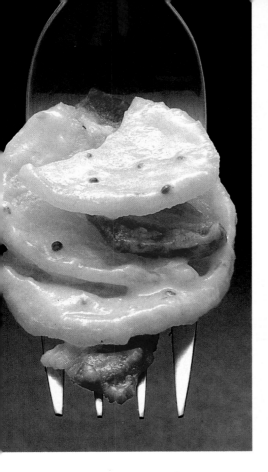

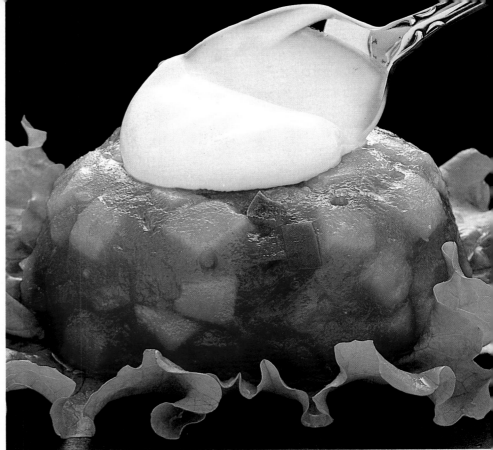

German Potato Salad ▲

6 slices bacon, cut into ½-in.
   pieces
1 pkg. (4¾ oz.) creamed
   potato mix
1 cup boiling water
1⅓ cups milk
  ¼ cup white vinegar
2 tablespoons sugar
  ¼ teaspoon celery seed

Serves 4 to·6

Place bacon in 2-qt. casserole;
cover. Microwave at High 5 to 6
minutes, or until crisp. Remove
to paper towel. Drain all but 2
tablespoons fat from casserole.
Stir potatoes and sauce mix,
boiling water and milk into fat;
cover. Microwave at High 5
minutes. Stir.

Reduce power to 50% (Medium). Microwave, uncovered, 8
to 10 minutes, or until potatoes
are almost tender, stirring after
half the time. Stir in vinegar,
sugar, celery seed and bacon.
Microwave at High 2 to 3
minutes, or until potatoes are
tender and mixture is heated.

Tomato Aspic ▲

½ cup hot water
1 teaspoon instant beef
   bouillon granules
1 can (12 oz.) tomato juice
1 pkg. (3 oz.) lemon-flavored
   gelatin
1 tablespoon plus 1½
   teaspoons white vinegar
½ teaspoon Worcestershire
   sauce
⅛ teaspoon black pepper

6 to 8 drops red pepper sauce
1 can (8 oz.) diced carrots,
   drained
½ cup frozen chopped green
   pepper
  ¼ cup frozen chopped onion or
   1 tablespoon dried
   onion flakes
⅓ cup mayonnaise or salad
   dressing

Serves 6

In 1-cup measure stir water and bouillon until bouillon dissolves.
Add enough tomato juice to measure 1 cup. Pour into 1-qt.
casserole or medium bowl; cover. Microwave at High 2 to 5
minutes, or until boiling. Stir in gelatin until dissolved. Mix in
remaining tomato juice, vinegar, Worcestershire sauce, black
pepper and red pepper sauce. Chill until slightly thickened. Stir in
vegetables. Pour into small mold or 6 individual molds. Chill until
firm. Serve with mayonnaise.

Sauces

Quick sauces add a personal touch to convenience meats, vegetables or desserts. Sauces can dress up a vegetable or create many dishes from one meat. For example, chicken can be sweet and sour, barbecued or creamed. With a few easy sauces you can add appetite appeal and variety to simple desserts of ice cream, plain cake, pudding or canned fruit.

◄ Cherry Dessert Sauce

1 can (21 oz.) cherry pie filling
¼ cup kirsch

Makes about 3 cups

Mix pie filling and kirsch in 1-qt. casserole or 4-cup measure. Microwave at High 2 to 4 minutes, or until heated, stirring after half the cooking time. Serve with ice cream or cake.

Variations:
Apple Dessert Sauce: Mix 1 can (21 oz.) apple pie filling, ½ teaspoon ground cinnamon and ¼ cup apple juice. Microwave as directed, above.

Blueberry Dessert Sauce: Mix 1 can (21 oz.) blueberry pie filling and ¼ cup prepared lemonade. Microwave as directed, above.

Raisin Sauce

1 jar (28 oz.) prepared mincemeat
½ cup apple juice

Makes about 4 cups

In 4-cup measure or medium bowl combine mincemeat and apple juice. Microwave at High 5 to 8 minutes, or until heated, stirring after half the time. Serve with ham or pork.

Variation:
Creamy Raisin Sauce: Blend ½ cup dairy sour cream into prepared raisin sauce. Serve over ice cream.

Prepared Ice Cream Toppings

Spoon desired amount of prepared ice cream topping (marshmallow, fudge, chocolate, pineapple, caramel, strawberry) into small bowl or 2-cup measure. Microwave at High as directed, below, until heated. Stir. Serve over ice cream or cake.

¼ cup topping: 25 to 35 seconds
½ cup topping: 40 to 60 seconds
1 cup topping: 1 to 1¼ minutes

Casserole & Vegetable Topping Suggestions

Top casseroles or vegetables with one of the following:

- Crushed potato chips
- Shoestring potatoes
- French fried onion rings
- Seasoned croutons
- Crushed crackers
- Shredded cheese

- Crushed seasoned bread stuffing mix tossed with melted butter
- Seasoned bread crumbs tossed with melted butter
- Toasted, slivered almonds

White Sauce

2 tablespoons butter or margarine
2 tablespoons all-purpose flour
¼ teaspoon salt
⅛ teaspoon pepper
1 cup milk

Makes 1 cup

Place butter in 4-cup measure or medium bowl. Microwave at High 30 to 60 seconds, or until melted. Blend in flour, salt and pepper. Add milk, stirring until smooth. Microwave at High 4 to 6 minutes, or until thickened, stirring after each minute with a wire whip.

Variations:
Cheese Sauce: Add ½ cup shredded Cheddar cheese to prepared white sauce, stirring until melted.

Mushroom Sauce: Add 1 teaspoon instant chicken bouillon granules and ½ teaspoon dried onion flakes to the melted butter. Blend in flour, seasonings and milk; microwave as directed. Stir in 1 can (4 oz.) sliced mushrooms, drained, before serving.

Mornay Sauce ▲

1 envelope (1 oz.) white sauce
   mix
¼ cup shredded Swiss cheese
2 tablespoons grated
   Parmesan cheese
½ teaspoon instant chicken
   bouillon granules
½ teaspoon dried parsley flakes
   Dash pepper

Makes about 1 cup

Prepare white sauce mix as
directed, page 120. Blend in
remaining ingredients.
Microwave at High 2 to 4
minutes, or until heated and
cheese melts, stirring after half
the time. Serve with vegetables,
eggs or poultry.

Salsa Sauce ▲

1 can (28 oz.) whole tomatoes,
   drained and juice reserved
1 can (4½ oz.) chopped green
   chilies
1 cup frozen chopped onion
2 tablespoons vegetable oil
2 to 3 teaspoons ground cumin
½ teaspoon crushed red
   pepper flakes

Makes about 4 cups

Pour reserved tomato juice into
2-qt. casserole. Chop tomatoes;
add to juice. Stir in remaining
ingredients. Microwave at High
8 to 12 minutes, or until flavors
are blended. Serve as a dip
with nacho chips or spoon over
tacos, enchiladas or burritos.

Sweet & Sour Sauce

1 jar (10 oz.) pineapple
   preserves
1 pkg. (1¾ oz.) sweet and
   sour sauce mix
½ cup water
2 tablespoons soy sauce

Makes 1½ cups

In 4-cup measure or medium
bowl mix preserves, sauce mix,
water, and soy sauce. Microwave at High 2 to 3 minutes, or
until slightly thickened and
flavors are blended. Serve with
chicken, pork or fish.

Tangy Barbecue Sauce ▲

1 bottle (12 oz.) chili sauce
½ cup catsup
2 tablespoons white vinegar
¼ teaspoon liquid smoke
2 tablespoons packed brown
    sugar
1 teaspoon prepared mustard
1 teaspoon dried onion flakes
¼ teaspoon garlic powder

Makes about 2 cups

Combine all ingredients in
4-cup measure or medium
bowl. Microwave at High 6 to 8
minutes, or until heated and
flavors are blended, stirring after
half the time. Serve over poultry
or spareribs.

Lemon Butter Sauce

½ cup butter or margarine
1 can (21 oz.) lemon pie filling
¼ cup lemon juice

Makes about 3¼ cups

Place butter in 1½-qt.
casserole. Microwave at High 1
to 1½ minutes, or until melted.
Add pie filling and lemon juice,
blending with wire whip.
Microwave at High 4 to 6
minutes, or until heated. Serve
over pound cake, gingerbread,
or angel food cake.

Variations:
Lemon-Lime Sauce: Substitute
lime juice for the lemon juice.

Lemon-Orange Sauce:
Substitute orange juice for the
lemon juice.

Caramel Butterscotch ▲
Sauce

½ bag (14 oz.) caramels,
    about 24
2¼ cups milk, divided
1 pkg. (3⅝ oz.) butterscotch
    pudding mix

Makes about 3 cups

Combine caramels and ¼ cup
milk in large bowl or 2-qt. casserole. Microwave at High 3 to
4 minutes, or until caramels are
melted and mixture is smooth,
stirring after each minute with a
wire whip. Combine remaining
milk and pudding mix. Blend
into melted caramels. Microwave at High 6 to 9 minutes, or
until boiling and thickened,
stirring every 3 minutes. Serve
over ice cream or cake.

Breads

In this section you'll find ways to dress up bakery breads and recipes for sweet or savory breads for breakfast, coffee break or dinner. Create them using baking mixes, refrigerated biscuits, or frozen yeast dough and convenience ingredients.

◄ Cheese French Bread

1 loaf (16 oz.) French bread
3 slices (¾ oz. each) American or Colby cheese, cut diagonally into 4 triangles
3 slices (¾ oz. each) Swiss or brick cheese, cut diagonally into 4 triangles

Makes 12 pieces

Cut loaf diagonally in half. Make diagonal cuts at 1½-in. intervals just to within ½ inch of bottom crust. Insert one triangle each of American and Swiss cheese between bread slices. Wrap each loaf half in paper towel. Microwave one at a time at 50% (Medium) 1 to 1½ minutes, or until cheese is softened and bread is warm to the touch. Repeat with remaining half.

Variations:
Garlic Cheese French Bread:
Omit cheese slices. Place 1 pkg. (3 oz.) cream cheese in small bowl. Microwave at 50% (Medium) 30 to 60 seconds, or until softened. Stir in 1 teaspoon dried chives and ½ teaspoon garlic powder. Spread between bread slices.

Parmesan French Bread: Omit cheese slices. Place ¼ cup butter or margarine in small bowl. Microwave at High 30 to 60 seconds, or until melted. Stir in ¼ cup grated Parmesan cheese. Brush between slices.

Spicy Carrot Bread ▲

1 pkg. (14½ oz.) gingerbread
   mix
1 can (8¼ oz.) crushed
   pineapple
1 jar (7½ oz.) carrot baby food

Makes 1 loaf

Line bottom of 8 × 5-in. loaf dish
with wax paper. In medium
bowl mix all ingredients. Spread
in dish. Shield ends of dish with
2-in. wide strips of foil. Place in
oven on inverted saucer.

Microwave at 50% (Medium) 9
minutes, rotating dish ¼ turn
every 3 minutes. Remove foil
shields. Increase power to High.
Microwave 3 to 8 minutes, or
until no unbaked batter can be
seen through bottom of dish.
Let stand directly on counter 5
to 10 minutes before removing
from dish.

Herb-Cheese Ring

3 tablespoons butter or
   margarine
1 pkg. (7½ oz.) refrigerated
   biscuits, 10-count
2 tablespoons grated American
   cheese food
2 teaspoons dried onion flakes
1 teaspoon dried parsley flakes
½ teaspoon paprika

Serves 4 to 6

Place butter in 9-in. ring baking
dish. Microwave at High 30 to
60 seconds, or until melted. Cut
each biscuit into quarters. In
plastic bag combine cheese,
onion flakes, parsley flakes and
paprika. Add half of the biscuit
quarters and shake to coat;
repeat. Arrange in baking dish.
Reduce power to 70% (Medium-
High). Microwave 4 to 6 minutes, or until springy to the
touch and no longer doughy,
rotating after half the time.

Bread From Frozen Dough

1 pkg. (32 oz.) frozen bread
   dough
2 tablespoons milk

Toppings: (use one)
¼ cup wheat germ
¼ to ½ cup cornmeal
¼ to ½ cup seasoned bread
   crumbs
2 to 3 tablespoons poppy
   seeds
½ cup quick-cooking rolled oats

Makes 1 loaf

Defrost frozen bread dough as
directed, page 103. Remove
defrosted dough from dish and
set aside. Coat bottom and
sides of greased loaf dish with
half of one of the toppings.
Brush defrosted loaf lightly with
milk and sprinkle with the other
half of the topping.

Place dough in loaf dish. Cover
loosely with plastic wrap. Set in
warm, draft-free place until
doubled in bulk. Place in oven
on inverted saucer. Microwave
at 50% (Medium) 6 minutes,
rotating after half the time.

Increase power to High.
Microwave 3 to 6 minutes, or
until light and springy and no
longer doughy, rotating every 2
minutes. Let stand in dish 2
minutes. Loosen edges and
invert onto cooling rack or
serving plate to cool.

Variation:
Dinner Rolls: Defrost 1 pkg.
(15 oz.) frozen dinner rolls as
directed, page 103. Brush each
roll lightly with milk and roll in
one of the above toppings to
coat. Arrange in 10-in. pie plate.
Cover loosely with plastic wrap.
Let rise until doubled in bulk.
Microwave at 50% (Medium) 8
to 12 minutes, or until light and
springy and no longer doughy,
rotating every 3 minutes.

Butterscotch Raisin Ring

1 pkg. (15 oz.) frozen honey
  wheat dinner rolls
1 pkg. (15 oz.) frozen white
  dinner rolls
¼ cup butter or margarine
1 pkg. (3⅝ oz.) butterscotch
  pudding mix
½ cup raisins

Makes 1 loaf

Defrost frozen rolls as directed in chart, page 103. Place butter in small dish. Microwave at High 1 to 1½ minutes, or until melted. Place pudding mix in medium bowl. Coat each roll with butter, then pudding mix.

Alternately arrange wheat rolls and white rolls in 8-cup ring baking dish, sprinkling raisins between layers. Cover loosely with plastic wrap. Place in warm, draft-free place until doubled in bulk, about 1 to 1½ hours. Remove plastic wrap.

Microwave at 50% (Medium) 6 minutes. Increase power to High. Microwave 4 to 5 minutes, or until light and springy to the touch and no longer doughy. Let stand 5 minutes.

Loosen edges with spatula. Invert onto heat-proof serving plate. Store any remaining bread in airtight container.

Variation:
Butterscotch Nut Ring:
Substitute ½ cup chopped pecans or walnuts for the raisins.

Pineapple-Cherry Ring

⅓ cup chopped maraschino
    cherries
1 can (8 oz.) crushed pine-
    apple, drained and 1 table-
    spoon juice reserved
2 pkgs. (7½ oz. each) refrig-
    erated buttermilk biscuits,
    10-count
2 tablespoons cinnamon-sugar
    or ½ teaspoon cinnamon
    plus 2 tablespoons sugar
¼ cup butter or margarine
½ cup packed brown sugar

Serves 6 to 8

How to Microwave Pineapple-Cherry Ring

Sprinkle chopped cherries and drained pineapple in 8- or 12-cup ring dish. Set aside.

Cut each biscuit into quarters. Place in medium bowl. Sprinkle with cinnamon-sugar. Toss lightly to coat.

Place biscuit pieces on top of fruit. Set aside. Mix butter, brown sugar and reserved pineapple juice in small bowl.

Microwave at High 1 to 1½ minutes, or until butter melts. Stir to blend. Microwave at High 1 to 2 minutes, or until bubbly. Pour evenly over biscuit pieces.

Place dish on inverted saucer. Microwave at 70% (Medium-High) 4½ to 7½ minutes, or until biscuits are springy to the touch, rotating 2 or 3 times.

Let stand on counter 3 minutes. Invert onto serving plate.

Maple Pecan Coffeecake

2 cups buttermilk baking mix
⅔ cup buttermilk
1 egg
2 tablespoons maple syrup

Topping:
½ cup packed brown sugar
¼ cup maple syrup
½ cup chopped pecans

Makes 9-in. coffeecake

In medium bowl combine baking mix, buttermilk, egg and 2 tablespoons maple syrup.

Prepare topping by mixing brown sugar and ¼ cup syrup in 9-in. round cake dish. Sprinkle with pecans. Spoon batter over topping. Microwave at 50% (Medium) 6 minutes, rotating after half the time. Increase power to High. Microwave 2 to 5 minutes, or until top springs back when lightly touched and wooden pick inserted in center comes out clean. Invert onto serving plate. Spread nuts evenly over top before serving.

Apple-Nut Pull Aparts ▶

½ cup packed brown sugar
¼ cup butter
1 tablespoon water
⅓ cup chopped walnuts
1 pkg. (10 oz.) refrigerated buttermilk fluffy biscuits, 10-count
1 cup chopped dried apples
¼ cup raisins, optional
1 teaspoon ground cinnamon

Serves 4 to 6

Place brown sugar, butter and water in 9-in. round baking dish. Microwave at High 1½ to 2 minutes, or until butter is melted. Stir to blend. Microwave at High 1 minute, or until mixture boils. Sprinkle with nuts.

Cut each biscuit into quarters. Place in medium bowl with remaining ingredients. Toss to coat biscuits with cinnamon.

Arrange biscuit-apple mixture evenly in baking dish. Microwave at 70% (Medium-High) 6 to 7 minutes, or until biscuits are light and springy to the touch, and no longer doughy. Invert onto serving plate.

Orange Rolls

1 pkg. (13¾ oz.) hot roll mix
3 tablespoons granulated
    sugar
1½ teaspoons ground
    cinnamon
2 tablespoons butter or
    margarine
½ cup orange marmalade
¼ cup packed dark brown
    sugar

Makes 1 dozen

How to Microwave Orange Rolls

Prepare roll mix as directed on package. Let dough rise as directed, or until doubled in bulk.

Punch down. In small bowl mix granulated sugar and cinnamon. Place butter in small dish. Microwave at High 30 to 60 seconds, or until melted.

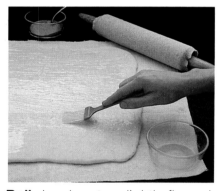

Roll dough out on lightly floured surface into 18 × 16-in. rectangle. Brush with melted butter. Sprinkle with cinnamon-sugar.

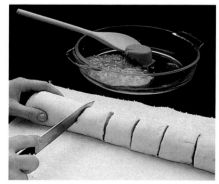

Roll up, starting with the long side. Pinch edges of seam together. Cut into 12 pieces. In 9-in. round baking dish mix marmalade and brown sugar.

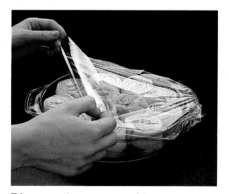

Place rolls on top of brown sugar-marmalade mixture. Cover with plastic wrap and let rise in a warm place until doubled in bulk. Place dish on inverted saucer in oven.

Microwave at 70% (Medium-High) 7 to 10 minutes, or until firm to touch, rotating ¼ turn every 2 minutes. Let stand 3 minutes. Invert onto plate.

Mexican Muffins ▲

1 pkg. (15 oz.) corn bread mix
1 envelope (1¼ oz.) taco
   seasoning mix
1 cup milk
1 egg
½ cup shredded Cheddar
   cheese

Makes 15 to 20 muffins

Line each of 6 custard cups or microwave muffin cups with 2 paper liners. In medium bowl mix all ingredients except cheese. Fill cups half full. Sprinkle each with about 1 teaspoon cheese. Arrange in ring in oven.

Microwave at High 1½ to 2 minutes, or until tops spring back when touched, rearranging after half the time. Remove from cups to wire rack. Moist spots will dry during cooling. Repeat with remaining muffins.

Easy Applesauce Muffins

2 cups buttermilk baking mix
1 cup chunk-style applesauce
½ cup raisins, optional
⅓ cup packed dark brown
   sugar
1 egg
1 teaspoon ground cinnamon
2 tablespoons cinnamon-sugar
   or ½ teaspoon cinnamon
   plus 2 tablespoons sugar

Makes 12 to 16 muffins

Line each of 6 custard cups or microwave muffin cups with 2 paper liners. In medium bowl mix all ingredients except cinnamon-sugar mixture. Fill cups half full. Sprinkle with cinnamon-sugar mixture. Arrange in ring in oven. Microwave at High 2½ to 3½ minutes, or until tops spring back when touched, rearranging after half the time. Remove from cups to wire rack. Moist spots will dry during cooling. Repeat with remaining muffins.

Savory Bread Stuffing

1 can (10¾ oz.) condensed
   chicken broth
1 can (10¾ oz.) condensed
   cream of chicken soup
1 can (5⅓ oz.) evaporated
   milk
6 cups unseasoned bread
   cubes
1 tablespoon dried onion
   flakes, optional
1 teaspoon dried parsley
   flakes, optional
⅛ teaspoon ground sage,
   optional

Serves 4 to 6

Blend soups and milk in large bowl. Mix in bread cubes, onion flakes, parsley and sage. Press into 8 × 8-in. baking dish. Place in oven on inverted saucer. Microwave at High 6 to 10 minutes, or until set, rotating 2 or 3 times. Stir after half the time, pressing stuffing firmly into dish after stirring.

Desserts

"What's for dessert?" A special dessert gives the simplest meal a memorable finish, and special needn't mean time and effort. In this section you'll find cakes, pies, fancied-up fruits and candies, made easily with convenience products, and so good you'll serve them on special occasions as well as on busy days.

◀ Cherry Chocolate Upside-Down Cake

2 tablespoons sugar
1 can (21 oz.) cherry pie filling, divided
1 pkg. (18½ to 18¾ oz.) devil's food cake mix (two-layer size)
1 teaspoon ground cinnamon
3 eggs
½ cup water
¼ cup vegetable oil

Makes one ring cake

Generously butter 12-cup ring cake dish. Sprinkle with sugar to coat sides and bottom. Spread half of the cherry pie filling in dish.

In large bowl combine remaining cherry pie filling, cake mix, cinnamon, eggs, water and oil. Beat at medium speed of electric mixer 3 minutes, scraping bowl occasionally. Pour into ring dish.

Microwave at 50% (Medium) 12 minutes, rotating every 3 minutes. Increase power to High. Microwave 1 to 8 minutes, or until cake springs back when lightly touched and begins to pull away from sides of dish. Let stand 10 minutes. Invert onto serving plate. Cool completely before slicing.

Fruit Spice Bundt Cake

2 tablespoons granulated sugar
1 pkg. (18½ to 18¾ oz.) spice cake mix (two-layer size)
3 eggs
¾ cup water
⅓ cup vegetable oil
1 cup chunk-style applesauce
1 pkg. (6 oz.) chopped, dried fruit with raisins
½ cup chopped walnuts

Frosting:

1 tablespoon butter or margarine
1 cup powdered sugar
½ teaspoon imitation maple flavoring
½ teaspoon vanilla
1 tablespoon hot water

Makes one ring cake

Generously butter 12-cup ring cake dish. Sprinkle with granulated sugar to coat sides and bottom.

In large bowl combine cake mix, eggs, water and oil. Beat at medium speed of electric mixer 3 minutes, scraping bowl occasionally. Add applesauce and fruit bits. Beat at low speed until well blended. Stir in nuts. Pour into ring dish.

Microwave at 50% (Medium) 12 minutes, rotating every 3 minutes. Increase power to High. Microwave 1 to 8 minutes, or until cake springs back when lightly touched and begins to pull away from sides. Let stand 10 minutes. Invert onto serving plate.

To prepare frosting, place butter in medium bowl. Microwave at High 15 to 30 seconds, or until melted. Stir in remaining ingredients until smooth. Drizzle over top of cake.

Apple Gingerbread Upside-Down Cake

½ can (21 oz.) apple pie filling
½ cup raisins
½ teaspoon ground cinnamon
1 pkg. (14 to 14½ oz.) ginger-
    bread mix

Makes 8 × 8-in. cake

In small bowl mix pie filling, raisins and cinnamon. Spread in 8 × 8-in. baking dish. Set aside.

Prepare gingerbread mix as directed on package. Pour evenly over apple mixture. Place dish in oven on inverted saucer. Microwave at 50% (Medium) 6 minutes, rotating after half the time. Increase power to High. Microwave 10 to 14 minutes, or until wooden pick inserted in center comes out clean, rotating ¼ turn every 3 minutes. Let stand on counter 5 minutes. Loosen edges and invert onto serving plate.

Peanut Butter Snack Cake

½ pkg. (31 oz.) peanut butter
    cookie mix
½ cup chunky-style peanut
    butter
 3 eggs
¼ cup honey
¼ cup milk
 1 pkg. (7½ oz.) fudge frosting
    mix

Makes 8 × 8-in. cake

Combine one cookie mix pouch with one flavor packet. Blend in peanut butter, eggs, honey and milk. Spread batter evenly in 8 × 8-in. baking dish. Place in oven on inverted saucer. Microwave at 50% (Medium) 12 minutes, rotating ¼ turn every 3 minutes. Increase power to High. Microwave 1 to 2 minutes, or until wooden pick inserted in center comes out clean. Cool. Prepare frosting as directed on package. Frost cooled cake.

Strawberry Chocolate ▲ Cream Cake

1 pkg. (9 oz.) devil's food cake mix (one-layer size)
1 pkg. (10 oz.) frozen sweetened strawberries
1 pkg. (3¾ oz.) instant vanilla pudding mix
1 container (4 oz.) frozen whipped dessert topping, defrosted

Makes 9-in. cake

Prepare cake mix as directed, page 140. Let stand 5 minutes. Invert onto serving plate. Cool. Defrost strawberries as directed, page 96. Drain; reserve juice.

Combine pudding mix and reserved juice in medium bowl. Beat at medium speed of electric mixer 2 minutes, or until mixture is blended and thickened. Stir in strawberries. Let stand 5 minutes to set. Fold in whipped topping.

Cut cake in half lengthwise to form two layers. Spoon one-third of strawberry filling onto bottom layer; top with other layer. Spread top and sides of cake with remaining filling. Refrigerate.

Apricot Orange Cobbler ▶

2 cups buttermilk baking mix
4 tablespoons sugar, divided
⅔ cup buttermilk
1 can (21 oz.) apricot pie filling
1 can (11 oz.) mandarin orange segments, drained
½ teaspoon ground cinnamon

Serves 6

In medium bowl mix buttermilk baking mix, 2 tablespoons sugar and buttermilk. Set aside.

In 1½-qt. casserole combine pie filling and oranges. Microwave at High 5 to 6 minutes, or until mixture is hot and bubbly, stirring after half the time.

Drop biscuit dough in 6 spoonfuls onto hot fruit. Mix remaining sugar and the cinnamon. Sprinkle evenly over biscuits. Microwave at High 4 to 6 minutes, or until top is springy and no longer doughy, rotating after half the time.

Variation:
Substitute 1 can (21 oz.) peach pie filling for apricot pie filling.

Raspberry Cherry Pie ▲

1 Graham Cracker Pie
   Crust, page 144
1 pkg. (10 oz.) frozen
   sweetened raspberries
1 can (21 oz.) cherry pie filling
1 tablespoon cornstarch

Makes 9-in. pie

Prepare 9-in. pie crust as directed. Set aside.

Defrost raspberries as directed, page 96. Drain. In 2-qt. casserole mix raspberries, pie filling and cornstarch. Microwave at High 5 to 7 minutes, or until mixture is clear and thickened. Pour into prepared crust. Chill.

Raspberry Cheesecake

1 pkg. (10 oz.) frozen
   sweetened raspberries
1 tablespoon cornstarch
¼ cup butter or margarine
1 cup graham cracker crumbs
2 tablespoons granulated
   sugar

1 pkg. (8 oz.) cream cheese
½ cup powdered sugar
1 container (4 oz.) frozen
   whipped dessert topping,
   defrosted

Makes 8 × 8-in. cake

Defrost raspberries as directed, page 96. Drain and reserve juice. In 4-cup measure mix reserved juice and cornstarch. Stir in raspberries. Microwave at High 4 to 8 minutes, or until clear and thickened, stirring every minute. Chill.

Place butter in 8 × 8-in. baking dish. Microwave at High 30 to 60 seconds, or until melted. Stir in graham cracker crumbs and granulated sugar. Press firmly into bottom of dish. Microwave at High 1½ minutes, rotating after 1 minute. Set aside.

Place cream cheese in medium bowl. Reduce power to 50% (Medium). Microwave 1 to 1½ minutes, or until softened. Add powdered sugar. Beat with electric mixer until blended. Fold in whipped topping. Spoon mixture into crust. Spread evenly. Top with raspberry topping. Refrigerate about 3 hours, or until set.

Coffee Pecan ▲ Ice Cream Pie

1 Graham Cracker Pie
   Crust, page 144
1 qt. vanilla ice cream
½ cup chopped pecans
2 tablespoons packed brown
   sugar
2 teaspoons instant coffee
   crystals
¼ teaspoon ground nutmeg

Makes 9-in. pie

Prepare 9-in. pie crust as directed. Set aside.

Place ice cream in large bowl. Divide into fourths. Microwave at 50% (Medium) 45 to 60 seconds, or until just softened. Do not let ice cream melt. Mix in remaining ingredients at low speed of electric mixer. Spoon into pie shell. Freeze 4 hours or until firm. Serve with chocolate syrup, if desired.

Sour Cream Pineapple Pie

1 pkg. (3⅛ oz.) vanilla pudding
   mix
1 can (15¼ oz.) crushed
   pineapple, packed in its
   own juice
1 cup dairy sour cream
¼ cup milk
½ teaspoon rum extract
1 pkg. (6 oz.) ready-to-fill
   graham cracker crust
1 container (4 oz.) frozen
   whipped dessert topping,
   defrosted

Makes 9-in. pie

In medium bowl mix pudding mix and undrained pineapple. Beat in sour cream and milk at low speed of electric mixer until smooth. Microwave at High 6 to 8 minutes, or until boiling, stirring after 2 minutes and then after every minute. Blend in rum extract. Let stand 5 minutes. Pour into pie crust. Cover with plastic wrap directly on surface. Chill at least 3 hours. Serve with whipped topping.

Variation:

Sour Cream Raisin Pie: To prepare filling, mix 1 pkg. (3⅛ oz.) vanilla pudding mix, 1 cup dairy sour cream, 1 cup milk, ¾ cup raisins, ½ teaspoon ground cinnamon and ⅛ teaspoon allspice. Microwave as directed, omitting rum extract.

◄ Fruit Pudding

1 can (20 oz.) chunk pineapple, drained and ¾ cup juice reserved
1 can (16 oz.) sliced peaches, drained and ¾ cup juice reserved
1 pkg. (3⅛ oz.) vanilla pudding mix
1 can (16 oz.) dark sweet pitted cherries, drained
2 medium bananas, sliced, optional

Serves 4 to 6

In medium bowl blend reserved pineapple and peach juices with pudding mix. Microwave at High 3 to 6 minutes, or until boiling, stirring after the first 2 minutes and then every minute. Cover with plastic wrap directly on surface. Let stand 1 hour. Stir in pineapple, peaches and cherries. Chill. Add bananas just before serving.

Variation:
Substitute 1 jar (16 oz.) maraschino cherries, drained, for the dark sweet cherries.

Raspberry Peach Compote

1 pkg. (10 oz.) frozen sweetened raspberries
2 cans (16 oz. each) sliced peaches, drained and ¼ cup juice reserved
1 tablespoon lemon juice
2 tablespoons cornstarch
2 tablespoons Amaretto

Serves 4

Defrost raspberries as directed, page 96. Place berries and juice in 1½-qt. casserole. In 1-cup measure or small bowl mix reserved peach juice, lemon juice, cornstarch and Amaretto. Blend cornstarch mixture into raspberries. Microwave at High 3 to 6 minutes, or until clear and thickened, stirring after each minute. Refrigerate. Stir in peaches just before serving.

Easy Rice Pudding ▲

1 cup instant rice
1 cup hot water
⅛ teaspoon salt
1 pkg. (3⅛ oz.) vanilla pudding
    mix
2 cups milk
½ teaspoon ground cinnamon
¼ cup raisins

               Serves 6

In 2-qt. casserole combine rice,
water and salt; cover. Microwave at High 5 to 6 minutes, or
until rice is tender and water is
absorbed, stirring after half the
cooking time. Let stand,
covered, 5 minutes.

Mix pudding mix with a small
amount of the milk. Stir into rice.
Stir in remaining milk. Mix in
cinnamon and raisins.
Microwave at High 5 to 7
minutes, or until boiling, stirring
after the first 2 minutes and then
after each minute. Let stand 5
minutes. Pour into serving
dishes. Chill.

Plum Pudding
With Hard Sauce

1 can (15 oz.) plum pudding

Sauce:
¼ cup butter or margarine,
    room temperature
¾ to 1 cup powdered sugar
¼ teaspoon vanilla
1 teaspoon water

               Serves 4

Remove pudding from can.
Place on serving plate; cover
with plastic wrap. Microwave at
High 2 to 3 minutes, or until
heated, rotating after half the
time. Set aside.

Place butter in medium bowl.
Beat at medium speed with
electric mixer 1 minute, or until
light and fluffy. Beat in sugar,
vanilla and water. Serve over
warm pudding.

Quick Chocolate Fondue ▲

1 can (16½ oz.) prepared
    chocolate frosting
1 to 2 tablespoons defrosted
    orange juice concentrate
    Fondue dippers (pound cake
    or angel food cake pieces,
    marshmallows, and fruits
    such as strawberries,
    banana slices and cherries)

        Makes about 2 cups

Empty frosting into 1-qt. serving
dish. Microwave at High 1 to
1½ minutes, or until melted. Stir
until smooth. Blend in orange
juice concentrate. Serve with
fondue dippers.

Variation:
Substitute ¼ cup Amaretto or
orange liqueur for the orange
juice concentrate.

Mock Toffee ▲

1 lb. butterscotch confectioners'
   candy coating
2 cups butter brickle chips
1 cup chocolate chips
½ cup chopped pecans

Makes about 3 lbs.

Place confectioners' candy
coating and butter brickle chips
in large bowl or 2-qt. casserole.
Microwave at 50% (Medium) 5
to 6 minutes, or until softened.
Stir until smooth and completely
melted. Spread to ¼-in.
thickness on wax paper. Cool
until hard.

Microwave chocolate chips at
50% (Medium) 3 to 5 minutes,
or until chips are shiny and
softened. Stir until melted.
Spread chocolate on set brickle;
sprinkle with chopped nuts.
Chill until set. Break into pieces.

Chocolate Marshmallow ▲ Squares

1 pkg. (12 oz.) semi-sweet
   chocolate chips or 1 pkg.
   (11½ oz.) milk chocolate
   chips
1 pkg. (6 oz.) butterscotch
   chips
½ cup peanut butter
1 pkg. (10 to 10½ oz.) mini-
   ature marshmallows
1 cup salted peanuts

Makes 20 pieces

In 3-qt. casserole combine
chocolate chips, butterscotch
chips and peanut butter.
Microwave at 50% (Medium)
3½ to 4½ minutes, or until chips
are softened, stirring after half
the time. Stir until smooth and
melted. Mix in marshmallows
and peanuts. Spread in lightly
greased 8 × 8-in. baking dish.
Cool completely before cutting.

Confetti Candy ▲

1 lb. white confectioners' candy
   coating
2 tablespoons vegetable
   shortening
1 pkg. (16 oz.) sugared gum
   drops

Makes 2 lbs.

Line 8 × 8-in. baking dish with
wax paper. Place confectioners'
candy and shortening in large
bowl or 2-qt. casserole.
Microwave at 50% (Medium) 3
to 5 minutes, or until pieces are
soft, stirring after first 3 minutes.
Stir in gum drops. Spread
mixture evenly in prepared dish.
Refrigerate until set. Cut into
1-in. pieces.

Variation:
Chocolate Coconut Candy:
Use 1 lb. chocolate
confectioners' candy coating,
1 cup dry roasted, salted peanuts and 1 cup flaked coconut.
Spread on wax paper-lined
baking sheet. Refrigerate until
set; break into pieces.

Peanut Butter Fudge ▶

2 cups peanut butter chips
1 cup chocolate chips
⅓ cup chopped peanuts
¼ cup butter or margarine
1 can (14 oz.) condensed milk

Makes 8 × 8-in. dish

Place all ingredients in 2-qt. mixing bowl. Microwave at 50% (Medium) 3 to 4 minutes, or until chips are melted, stirring once. Stir to blend. Pour into 8 × 8-in. baking dish. Chill until set. Cut into squares.

Chocolate Crunch Cups ▶

1 pkg. (11½ oz.) butterscotch chips
1 pkg. (6 oz.) milk chocolate chips
1½ cups dry roasted salted peanuts
1 cup crushed ripple potato chips

Makes 1½ lbs.

In medium bowl combine butterscotch and milk chocolate chips. Microwave at 50% (Medium) 2 to 4 minutes, or until softened, stirring each minute. Stir in peanuts and potato chips. Drop by spoonfuls onto wax paper or into paper candy cups. Chill until set.

Raisin Bran Chewies ▶

½ bag (14 oz.) caramels, about 24
1 can (5 oz.) evaporated milk
3½ cups raisin bran cereal

Makes 2½ dozen

In large bowl combine the caramels and evaporated milk. Microwave at High 5 to 9 minutes, or until boiling, stirring after each minute. Stir in cereal. Drop by teaspoonfuls onto wax paper. Chill until firm.

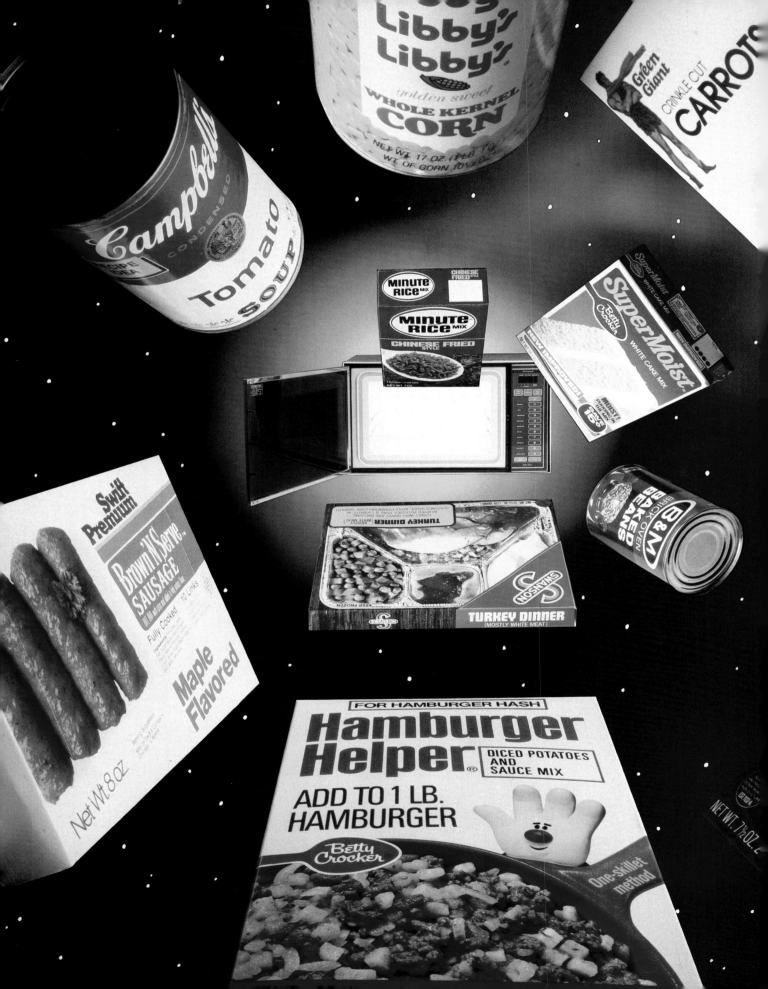

Basic Directions for Convenience Foods

Most convenience foods can be prepared in·the microwave oven. This section provides step-by-step directions and comprehensive charts for frozen, canned and refrigerated foods, dry mixes, and fast foods.

NET WT. 10 OZ.

IN THE FLAVOR-TIGHT POUCH

NET WT. 9.5 OZ. (269 g)

Pillsbury

8 QUICK

CINNAMON ROLLS

WITH ICING

Stouffer's Ham & Swiss Cheese Crepes with Cream Sauce

FOODS
139   Keep frozen

Frozen Foods

A variety of frozen foods packaged in boxes, pouches, and foil or paperboard trays are widely available. This section presents defrosting and cooking information on them.

Frozen TV Dinners

TV dinners can be microwaved in their foil trays. The tray shields food on the bottom, so it heats only from the top. If the tray has a foil cover, remove it, or the food won't heat.

Center tray in oven; leave 1 inch of space between foil and oven walls. This prevents electrical arcing, which can occur if metal is too close to oven walls. Arcing should be avoided because it can damage oven walls.

Cake-like desserts and breads should be removed from the tray and microwaved separately; they heat in just seconds.

How to Microwave Frozen TV Dinners

Remove tray from box; remove foil cover. If tray is covered by plastic film, treat as directed by manufacturer. Remove cake-like desserts or breads from tray. Set aside. If dinner contains egg roll, place paper towel under roll to absorb moisture; remove egg roll after first 5 minutes of microwaving.

Cover tray with wax paper; center in oven. Microwave at High for minimum time as directed in chart, rotating ¼ turn every 3 minutes.

Stir dinner or turn over any large pieces, if possible. Microwave remaining time, or until dinner is heated.

Wrap bread in paper towel; microwave at High 10 to 15 seconds, or until warm to touch. Place dessert in custard cup; microwave at High 30 to 60 seconds.

Frozen TV Dinner Chart

Type of Tray	Package Weight	Microwave Time at High	Procedure
2-compartment trays	12 to 13¼ oz.	6-7 min.	Follow photo directions, above.
3-compartment trays	8¾ to 16 oz.	6-12 min.	Follow photo directions, above.
4-compartment trays	10¼ to 22 oz.	7-12 min.	Follow photo directions, above.

Frozen Entrées
& Side Dishes

Frozen entrées and side dishes are packaged in foil and paperboard trays, poly bags and pouches. The pouches are either single, with all ingredients in the same pouch, or double, with sauce in one pouch and rice or pasta in another. The time and techniques needed to microwave frozen entrées and side dishes depend primarily on the weight and type of package. Some popular foods are available in several types of packages. To use the chart, look for the type of package, not the food item.

How to Microwave Single Pouches

Cut large "X" in one side of pouch. Place pouch cut side down in 1- to 1½-qt. casserole.

Microwave at High as directed in chart, below, until food is heated.

Lift opposite corners of pouch to empty food into casserole. Stir before serving.

How to Microwave Double Pouches

Cut large "X" in one side of each pouch. Place sauce pouch, cut side down, in 1-qt. casserole. Microwave at High as directed in chart, below.

Place rice or pasta pouch, cut side up, on top of sauce pouch. Microwave at High remaining time, or until rice or pasta pouch is heated, stirring once.

Serve by inverting top pouch onto plate. Empty sauce pouch into casserole. Stir. Spoon over rice or pasta.

Frozen Foods in Pouches Chart

Type of Pouch	Package Weight	Microwave Time at High	Procedure
Single Pouches	4 to 5 oz.	2-4 min.	Follow photo directions for single pouches, above.
	8 to 12 oz.	4-8 min.	
Double Pouches	9½ to 14 oz.	2 min. (sauce) 3-6 min. (rice or pasta)	Follow photo directions for double pouches, above.
Poly Bags Lasagna 4 individual squares	30 oz.	High: 5 min., then 50% (Med.): 20-25 min.	Remove lasagna from bag. Place in 12 × 8-in. baking dish. Add 2 cups or 1 jar (16 oz.) Italian sauce. Cover with plastic wrap. Microwave at High. Turn pieces over and rotate dish ½ turn. Reduce power. Microwave until center is heated, rotating after half the time.
Ravioli	30 oz.	High: 5 min., then 50% (Med.): 7-14 min.	Remove ravioli from bag. Place in 12 × 8-in. baking dish. Add 1 jar (16 oz.) Italian sauce. Cover with plastic wrap. Microwave at High. Stir. Reduce power. Microwave until heated, stirring twice during cooking.

How to Microwave Frozen Foods in Trays

Foil Tray. Remove food from tray. Place in casserole. Cover with wax paper.

Paperboard Tray. Entrées can be microwaved in paperboard tray. Follow manufacturer's directions for treatment of plastic film.

Microwave as directed in chart, below. After half the time, stir food in casserole or rotate paperboard tray ¼ turn. Microwave until heated.

Frozen Foods in Trays Chart

Item	Package Weight	Microwave Time	Procedure
Entrées & Side Dishes All except those listed opposite	6¼ to 9½ oz.	High: 3½ to 7 min.	Follow photo directions, above.
	10 to 13 oz.	High: 3 min., then 50% (Med.): 6-9 min.	
	14 to 21 oz.	High: 5 min., then 50% (Med.): 5-15 min.	

Item	Package Weight	Microwave Time at High	Procedure
Exceptions:			
Family Size Entrées	30 to 32 oz.	32-40 min.	Preheat browning grill at High 5 minutes. Loosen lid from pan; if lid is foil-lined, replace with wax paper cut to same size. Place pan on browning grill. Microwave until heated, rotating pan ½ turn after half the time. Let stand, covered, 5 minutes.
Beef Enchiladas	9⅕ oz.	5-9 min.	Arrange enchiladas in 8 × 8-in. baking dish. Top with 1 cup enchilada sauce and onion as directed on package. Cover with wax paper. Microwave until heated, rearranging enchiladas and rotating dish after half the time.
Tamales 1 tamale 2 tamales 4 tamales	16 oz.	 2-3 min. 3-6 min. 6-8 min.	Place tamales in 8 × 8-in. baking dish, seam side down. Microwave until heated, rearranging tamales and rotating dish after half the time.
Crêpes	6¼ to 9½ oz.	3-5 min.	Transfer crêpes from foil pan to serving plate. Cover with plastic wrap. Microwave until heated, rotating dish 2 or 3 times. If package contains sauce, place frozen sauce packet in hot water to defrost. Pour over crêpes during last minute of cooking.
Chili	14 oz.	5-9 min.	Transfer chili from package to 1-qt. casserole. Cover. Microwave until heated, stirring to break apart after half the time.
Soufflé	12 oz.	5-8 min.	Transfer soufflé from package to 1-qt. casserole or baking dish similar to the package size. Cover. Microwave until heated, stirring after half the time.
Baked Beans	16 oz. 32 oz.	5-6 min. 10-12 min.	Transfer beans from foil pan to 1½- or 3-qt. casserole. Cover. Microwave until heated, stirring after half the time.
Seasoned Rice Dishes	11 oz.	5-6 min.	In 1½-qt. casserole combine seasonings, water and butter as directed on package. Add rice. Cover. Microwave until heated, stirring after half the time. Let stand, covered, 2 minutes.

Frozen Convenience Meats & Fish

Some convenience meats are fully cooked and only need microwaving until heated through. Others are uncooked, but have been boned, seasoned or breaded for you. Be sure to choose fish sticks and patties with a toasted bread crumb coating. These convenience meat, fish and poultry products can be microwaved without defrosting.

Frozen Convenience Meat & Fish Chart

Item	Amount	Microwave Time at High	Procedure
Turkey Roast	2 lbs.	High: 5 min., then 50% (Med.): 15-35 min.	Set aside gravy packet. Transfer roast from foil pan to 9 × 5-in. loaf dish. Cover with wax paper. Microwave at High. Rotate ¼ turn. Reduce power. Microwave until internal temperature reaches 175°, rotating 2 or 3 times. Let stand 5 minutes. If preparing gravy, remove roast from dish. Reduce water by ¼ cup. Add gravy mix and water to drippings. Microwave at High 6 to 8 minutes, or until thickened, stirring every 2 minutes.
Precooked Fried Chicken	2 to 3 pieces	2½-5 min.	Separate and arrange on roasting rack with meatiest portions to outside of dish. Cover with paper towel. Rearrange, but do not turn over, after half the time. Let stand 2 to 3 minutes on paper towel-lined plate covered with paper towel. Microwave 60 oz. package half box at a time.
	4 pieces	4-6½ min.	
	16 oz. (5 to 7 pieces)	9-11 min.	
	32 oz. (9 to 11 pieces)	15-17 min.	
	60 oz. (½ box)	15-17 min.	
Chicken Kiev or Cordon Bleu	12 oz.	5-8 min.	Remove plastic inner wrap. Place on roasting rack or trivet. Rotate dish ½ turn after half the time.

Item	Amount		Microwave Time at High	Procedure
Breaded Fish Sticks & Patties (Toasted Bread Crumb Coating only)	Sticks:	4	2-2½ min.	Preheat browning dish at High 5 minutes. Add 1 tablespoon vegetable oil, if desired. Add fish, pressing down with spatula to brown. Microwave until center is opaque, and fish flakes easily with a fork, rotating dish and turning fish over after half the time.
		6	2-3 min.	
		8	2-4 min.	
	Patties:	2	4-4½ min.	
		4	4-6 min.	
Fish Fillets	Any size		50% (Med.): 3-9 min./lb., then High: 5-7 min./lb.	Place fillets in baking dish with thickest portions to outside. Microwave at 50% (Medium) until defrosted, rearranging after half the time. Let stand 5 minutes. Increase power. Add lemon juice and butter, if desired. Cover loosely with plastic wrap. Microwave until fish flakes easily, rearranging after half the time.
Taco Filling	16 oz.		50% (Med.): 5-6 min., then High: 2-4 min.	Microwave in wrapper at 50% (Medium). Remove wrapper after first minute. Place filling in 1½-qt. casserole. Cover with wax paper. Microwave until meat can be broken apart, stirring every 2 minutes. Increase power to High. Microwave until meat is no longer pink, stirring to break apart after half the time.

Frozen
Pizza

Microwave Pizza Utensils

Use & Care

Preheat browner at High 5 minutes, or elevated pizza stone 7½ minutes.

Use pot holders to remove utensil; place on heat resistant pad.

Remove pizza to a board or plate for cutting and serving. The porous stone can absorb moisture or fat from sauce or toppings; knife cuts can mar the surface of browner.

Dry pizza stone thoroughly before reuse.

Follow manufacturer's directions for cleaning utensil.

Pizza Stone. Made of porous ceramic, it is similar to conventional baking stones. Look for the coating on the bottom to identify it as a microwave utensil. Since it becomes very hot, elevate it on a roasting rack to protect oven. The stone can be used to microwave egg rolls and cookies or conventionally.

Pizza Browner. Made of pyroceram, it is similar to a microwave browning dish. A bottom rim elevates the utensil during microwaving. This rim also protects counters from heat. The browner can be used to microwave egg rolls, but *do not* use it for cookies or conventional baking.

How to Microwave Frozen Pizza

Remove pizza from package. Brush ice crystals from bottom of pizza. Preheat pizza stone or browner as directed, above.

Place pizza on preheated stone or browner. Microwave at High as directed in chart, below, until heated and crisp.

Check bottom for doneness. Reheat stone at High 3½ minutes or browner 4 minutes before doing another pizza.

Frozen Pizza Chart

Item	Package Weight	Microwave Time at High	Procedure
Pizza			
8- to 9-in.	8 to 9 oz.	4-6 min.	Follow photo directions, above.
10- to 11-in.	11 to 15 oz.	5-7 min.	
11-in.	15 to 18 oz.	6-8 min.	
11- to 12-in.	20 to 25 oz.	7-11 min.	
Two Individual Pizzas	10⁹⁄₁₀ oz.	6-8 min.	Follow photo directions, above. Microwave one or two pizzas at a time.
Pizza on French Bread	10¼ to 12⅜ oz.	7-8 min.	Follow photo directions, above. Microwave one or two pizzas at a time.
Mini Pizzas 4-, 6-, 8-pack	7¼ oz.	3-5 min.	Follow photo directions, above. Microwave one or more pizzas at a time.
	15½ to 16 oz.	6-7 min.	

Frozen Sandwiches

Frozen Sandwich Chart

Item	Amount	Microwave Time at High	Procedure
Meat & Cheese Sandwiches 7½ to 9 oz. each All except those listed below	1 2	1½-2 min. 1¾-2½ min.	Remove outer wrapper. Place on paper towel-lined plate or assemble sandwich as directed and wrap in paper towel. Microwave until heated.
Exceptions: Italian Meatball or Sausage Sandwich 7¾ to 8¼ oz.	1	5-8 min. (meat) 10-20 sec. (bread)	Place meat and sauce in 1-qt. casserole. Microwave until heated, rearranging meatballs after half the time. Set aside. Wrap bread in paper towel. Microwave until warm to touch. Assemble sandwich as directed on package.
Burritos 3 to 5 oz. each	1 2 4	1-2½ min. 2½-4 min. 4-7½ min.	Cut off one end of package. Place on oven floor. Microwave until heated, turning over after half the time. Remove from bag.

Frozen Appetizers

Use a microwave pizza stone, pizza browner or browning dish to prepare frozen appetizers. These utensils become hot during preheating which keeps the surface of the appetizers crisp. A regular casserole or plate will not produce the same results.

How to Microwave Frozen Pizza Rolls & Egg Rolls

Preheat microwave pizza browner at High 6 minutes, or elevated microwave pizza stone at High 9 minutes.

Arrange egg rolls or pizza rolls on stone or browner.

Microwave at High 3 to 6 minutes, or until crisp, turning over after every minute. Reheat utensil between batches.

Frozen Fruit

Your microwave oven adds to the convenience of frozen fruits by defrosting them rapidly. Fruits frozen in syrup can be defrosted at High because the syrup shields them and prevents cooking. Use 50% (Medium) for unsugared fruits. In either case, defrost only until a few pieces feel warm, then let stand to defrost completely.

Defrosting Frozen Fruit Chart

Type of Package	Amount	Microwave Time	Procedure
Poly Bags		50% (Med):	Measure amount needed into 1- to 2-qt. casserole. Microwave until a few pieces feel warm, stirring once or twice. Let stand 5 minutes.
	1 cup	1-3 min.	
	2 cups	2½-5 min.	
	4 cups	5-8 min.	
Quick-Thaw Pouches	10 oz.	High: 2-3 min.	Flex pouch to break up fruit. Cut large "X" in pouch. Place cut side down in 1-qt. casserole or serving dish. Microwave until outer fruit feels slightly warm. Empty fruit into dish. Stir; let stand 5 minutes.
Boxes		High:	If box has metal ends, remove one end and set package upright in oven. Place all-paper box unopened in bowl. Microwave until outer berries or paper carton feel slightly warm. Let stand 10 to 12 minutes. Pour fruit into bowl. Stir carefully to break up.
	10 oz.	2 min.	
	16 oz.	2-3 min.	
Plastic Containers	16 oz.	High: 3 min., then 30-60 sec.	Run hot water over container to loosen fruit. Place fruit in bowl. Microwave 3 minutes. Let stand 5 minutes; break apart. Microwave 30 to 60 seconds, or until able to separate. Let stand 5 minutes.

A wide variety of vegetables are available frozen in boxes, poly bags and pouches. Microwaving time varies with the amount and desired texture of the vegetable. The times suggested in the chart, page 99, are for vegetables which are tender, but still crisp. In general, small pieces will cook faster than the larger, denser pieces.

How to Microwave Frozen Vegetables in Box or Poly Bag

Place frozen vegetables in 1-qt. casserole with 2 tablespoons water. Cover.

Microwave at High as directed in chart, opposite, until vegetables are heated and tender-crisp, stirring once.

Let stand, covered, 2 to 3 minutes to equalize heat and complete cooking.

How to Microwave Frozen Vegetables in Pouch

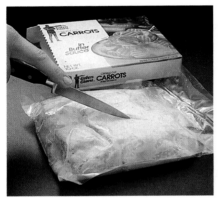

Flex pouch to break apart vegetables. Cut large "X" in one side of pouch.

Place cut side down in 1-qt. casserole or serving dish.

Microwave at High as directed in chart, opposite, until center of pouch is hot to touch. Empty vegetables into dish; stir.

How to Microwave Frozen Stir-Fry Vegetables

Preheat microwave browning dish at High 3 minutes. Spread vegetables in dish.

Pour 1 tablespoon vegetable oil over vegetables and sprinkle with seasonings from packet.

Stir quickly to coat pieces. Cover. Microwave at High as directed in chart, until vegetables are heated and tender-crisp.

Frozen Vegetable Chart

Item	Package Weight	Microwave Time at High	Procedure
Vegetables			
In box or poly bag	8 to 10 oz. box or 2 cups	4-7 min.	Follow box photo directions, opposite. If package contains sauce, place frozen sauce packet in hot water to defrost. Pour over cooked vegetables.
In cheese sauce	10 oz. pouch	6-8 min.	Follow pouch photo directions, opposite.
In butter sauce	9 oz. pouch	5-7 min.	Follow pouch photo directions, opposite.
Exceptions:			
Greens: Spinach, Collard, Kale, Turnip	10 oz. box	7-10 min.	Follow box photo directions, opposite.
Pea Pods	6 oz. box	3-4 min.	Follow box photo directions, opposite.
Black-eyed Peas	10 oz. box	8-9 min.	Follow box photo directions, opposite.
Corn on the Cob 1 ear 2 ears 4 ears		3-4½ min. 6½-8½ min. 12-14 min.	Place ears in large dish with 2 table-spoons water. Cover tightly with plastic wrap. Turn over and rearrange once.
Stuffed Potatoes	10 oz. box	6-8 min.	Place in 1-qt. casserole. Cover loosely. Rotate dish ¼ turn after 3 minutes.
Candied Sweet Potatoes	12 oz. box	4-6 min.	Microwave in box with front flap opened, or place in 1-qt. covered casserole. Stir or turn over box after half the time.
Vegetable Combinations			
In box or poly bag	8 to 10 oz. box or 2 cups	4-7 min.	Follow box photo directions, opposite.
In seasoned sauce	10 oz. box	6-8 min.	Omit water. Place vegetables and butter as directed on package in 1½-qt. casserole. Cover. Stir to break up after half the time. Let stand, covered, 2 minutes.
In cream sauce	8 to 10 oz. box	5-6 min.	Place vegetables in 1½-qt. casserole with 1 tablespoon butter and milk or water as directed on package. Stir after half the time until sauce is smooth. Let stand, covered, 2 minutes.
In butter sauce	9 to 10 oz. pouch	5-7 min.	Follow pouch photo directions, opposite.
In cheese sauce	10 oz. pouch	6-8 min.	Follow pouch photo directions, opposite.
Stir-Fry combination	10 oz. box	4-5 min.	Follow stir-fry photo directions, opposite.

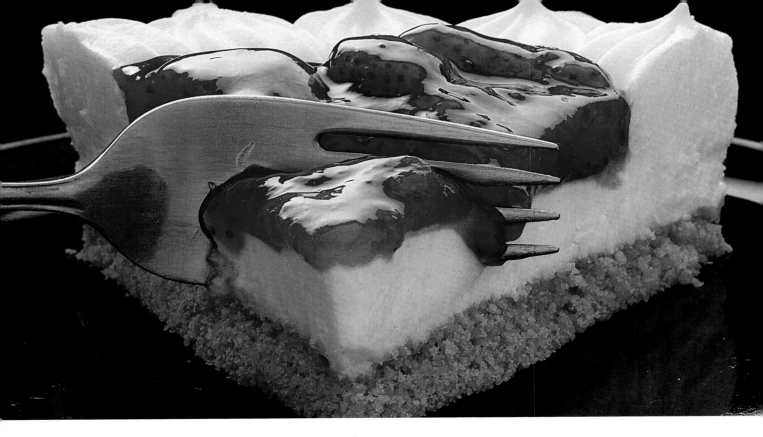

Frozen Desserts

Most frozen desserts are delicate, and should be defrosted at 30% (Medium-Low) to avoid melting icings or sensitive fillings. The exceptions are coffee cakes and fruit pies, which are defrosted at 50% (Medium). Frozen pie crust defrosts at 50% (Medium) in less than a minute and can then be microwaved at High.

How to Defrost Frozen Desserts

Remove dessert from box; transfer to serving dish or plate if directed in chart, opposite.

Microwave until wooden pick inserted in center meets no resistance, rotating dish 2 or 3 times. If icing begins to soften, remove from oven; let stand.

How to Microwave Frozen Pie Crust

Transfer frozen crust from foil pan to 9-in. glass pie plate. Microwave at 50% (Medium) 30 to 60 seconds, or until defrosted.

Form crust to shape of pie plate. Crimp crust edges. Prick crust with fork at bend of plate, sides and bottom.

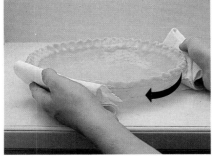

Microwave at High as directed in chart, opposite, or until crust is dry and opaque, rotating dish after half the time.

Defrosting Frozen Dessert Chart

Item	Package Weight	Defrost Time at 30% (Medium-Low)	Procedure
Layer Cake with Icing	10 to 13¾ oz. 15¾ to 18 oz. 21 to 24 oz.	1-3½ min. 1½-4 min. 3½-6 min.	Follow dessert photo directions, opposite. Transfer one-layer cake from foil pan to serving plate. Two- and three-layer cakes can be defrosted on styrofoam base or serving plate. Let stand 15 to 20 minutes.
Pound Cake	9½ to 12⅞ oz. 16 oz.	¾-1½ min. 1-2 min.	Follow dessert photo directions, opposite. Use serving plate. Let stand 5 minutes.
Crumb Cake 1 cake 6 cakes	10¼ to 10½ oz.	25-30 sec. 1-1½ min.	Follow dessert photo directions, opposite. Use serving plate or defrost cakes in inner plastic tray.
Cheesecake	10 oz. 17 to 19 oz.	1-3½ min. 1½-4 min.	Follow dessert photo directions, opposite. Use serving plate. Let stand 10 to 15 minutes.
Individual Cheesecake	6 oz.	1-2½ min.	Follow dessert photo directions, opposite. Remove plastic cover. Defrost in plastic pan, checking after every minute.
Brownies	13 oz.	1-3 min.	Follow dessert photo directions, opposite. Use paper towel-lined plate. Let stand 5 minutes.
Cream Pie	14 oz.	¾-2 min.	Follow dessert photo directions, opposite. Use glass pie plate. Let stand 5 minutes.
Individual Cream Pie	3.5 oz.	1-2½ min.	Follow dessert photo directions, opposite. Remove plastic cover. Defrost in plastic pan, checking after every minute.
Coffee Cake	6½ to 15 oz.	50% (Med.): 1-4 min.	Follow dessert photo directions, opposite. Use paper towel-lined plate. Let stand 5 minutes.
Double Crust Pie	26 to 40 oz.	50% (Med.): 5½-9 min./lb.	To defrost, follow dessert photo directions, opposite. Use glass pie plate. Rotate after half the time. Bake conventionally as directed on package for one-third to one-half the suggested time.
Pie Crust	5 to 6 oz.	50% (Med): 30-60 sec. High: 2-3½ min.	Follow pie crust photo directions, opposite. If adding sweet filling, brush defrosted crust with vanilla. Microwave as directed. Fill. If adding a liquid filling, brush microwaved crust with slightly beaten egg yolk. Microwave at High 30 to 60 seconds, or until egg is set. Fill.

Frozen Bakery

How to Defrost Frozen Doughnuts & Rolls

Most frozen bakery is ready to serve after defrosting, except frozen bread dough and dinner roll dough, which must be proofed and baked. Place baked goods on a paper towel to absorb excess moisture.

Arrange doughnuts or sweet rolls on paper towel-lined baking sheet or serving dish.

Microwave at High as directed in chart, opposite, until warm to the touch, rotating dish after half the time.

How to Defrost Frozen Bread Dough

Measure 1 to 1½ cups water into 12 × 8-in. baking dish. Microwave at High until boiling. Grease an 8 × 4-in. or 9 × 5-in. loaf dish. Butter frozen loaf on all sides.

Place loaf in loaf dish; set in hot water. Cover with wax paper. Microwave at 50% (Medium) 2 minutes, rotating ¼ turn each minute. Turn loaf over. Microwave at High 2 minutes, rotating ¼ turn every minute.

Let stand 10 minutes. Dough should be defrosted and slightly warm. If necessary, continue to microwave 1 minute at a time until defrosted. Proof and bake as directed, page 66.

Defrosting Frozen Bakery Chart

Item	Amount	Microwave Time at High	Procedure
Muffins 11½ to 12½ oz.	1 2 4 6	30-45 sec. 45-60 sec. 1-2 min. 2-3 min.	Place muffins directly on oven floor or leave in paperboard tray. Microwave until warm to touch. When microwaving 4 to 6 muffins, rearrange after half the time.
Heat & Serve Biscuits 12 oz. (12-count)	1 2 4 12	20-30 sec. 30-45 sec. 1¼-1¾ min. 2¼-3 min.	Follow photo directions for doughnuts, opposite, rotating every 30 seconds.
Glazed & Cake Doughnuts 9 to 12 oz.	1 2 4 to 6	10-15 sec. 20-30 sec. 30-60 sec.	Follow photo directions for doughnuts, opposite.
Cream-Filled Bavarian Doughnuts 12 oz.	6	50% (Med.): 2½-3 min.	Arrange on paper towel-lined plate. Microwave only until defrosted, rotating every minute. Do not overheat. Let stand 15 minutes to complete defrosting.
Jelly-Filled Doughnuts 11 oz.	1 2 4 to 6	30-40 sec. 45-60 sec. ¾-1¾ min.	Follow photo directions for doughnuts, opposite. Let stand 15 minutes.
Mini Doughnuts 10 to 14 oz. (18- or 24-count)	2 4 9 to 12	15-30 sec. 35-40 sec. 1-1½ min.	Follow photo directions for doughnuts, opposite.
Doughnut Holes 7¾ oz.	10	1-1¾ min.	Follow photo directions for doughnuts, opposite.
Danish Rolls 7¾ oz.	1 2 4 to 6	10-15 sec. 20-30 sec. 30-60 sec.	Follow photo directions for doughnuts, opposite.
Sweet Rolls 8¼ to 10 oz. 10½ oz.	9 9	45-60 sec. 1½-3 min.	Invert rolls onto serving plate. Microwave until warm to touch, rotating dish after half the time.
Bread Dough 32 oz.	1 loaf	50% (Med.): 2 min., then High: 2 min.	Follow photo directions for bread dough, opposite.
Dinner Roll Dough 15 oz.	12	50% (Med.): 2-3 min.	Place rolls in greased 10-in. pie plate. Cover with wax paper. Microwave until warm to touch, rotating after every minute and turning rolls over after half the time. Let stand 10 minutes. Proof and bake as directed, page 66.

Frozen Breakfast Dishes

Convenience foods, prepared in the microwave oven, are especially welcome on a busy morning. A hot, easy breakfast can be ready in just minutes.

Frozen Breakfast Dishes Chart

Item	Package Weight	Microwave Time at High	Procedure
TV Breakfast	4½ to 6 oz. 6¼ oz. 8 oz.	2-2½ min. 3½-4 min. 6-7 min.	Follow photo directions for frozen foods in paperboard trays, page 88.
Bulk Pork Sausage	12 to 16 oz.	50% (Med.): 3 min.	Defrost in wrapper, turning over once. Remove wrapper. Slice into patties; let stand 20 to 30 minutes, or until center is no longer icy. Microwave as directed, page 148.
Egg Substitutes	4 oz. carton 8.5 oz. carton	50% (Med.): 1½-2 min. 50% (Med.): 2-3 min.	**To Defrost:** Open spout. Place carton in oven. Microwave until stirrable. Let stand 1 to 2 minutes. Defrosted egg substitutes can be stored in refrigerator.
	1 egg 2 eggs 4 eggs	High: 30-60 sec. High: 1¼-1½ min. High: 1½-3 min.	**To Microwave:** Pour desired amount into 1- or 2-cup measure. Microwave until eggs begin to set, stirring every 30 seconds, pushing cooked portions to center. Remove when eggs are still soft and moist. Let stand 1 to 2 minutes. Eggs will firm up while standing. Stir before serving.
French Toast	9 oz.	1-1½ min.	Place 2 slices French toast on serving plate. Microwave until warm to touch. Top with butter and syrup before microwaving, if desired.
Juice Concentrate	6 oz. 12 oz.	½-1½ min. 1-2½ min.	Remove top and metal rim. Place in oven. Microwave until softened, but not warm. Prepare as directed.

Libby's
Libby's
Libby's

S
CA

NET W

Green Giant
Golden Corn
Whole
Kernel

NET WT. 17 OZ (1 LB. 1 O
WT. OF CORN 10.5 OZ

Canned Main Dishes

Canned main dishes are fully cooked and heated from room temperature, so microwaving time is based on quantity and type of food. The times and techniques are the same for similar can weights and types of main dishes. Chow mein packed in a single can is included in the general directions. Exceptions are chow mein which is packed with meat sauce in one can and vegetables in another, and canned tamales or enchiladas.

How to Microwave Canned Main Dishes

Place food in dish or casserole as directed in chart, opposite. Cover single servings with paper towel to prevent spatters. Use casserole lid to cover larger amounts.

Microwave at High as directed in chart until heated, stirring after half the time.

Canned Main Dish Chart

Item	Can Weight	Microwave Time at High	Procedure
Main Dishes All except those listed below			Follow photo directions, opposite.
	7 to 8 oz.	1½-2½ min.	Use 15-oz. individual bowl.
	10½ to 16 oz.	2-5 min.	Use 1-qt. covered casserole.
	16 to 32 oz.	3-6 min.	Use 1-qt. covered casserole.
	40 oz.	6-7 min.	Use 2-qt. covered casserole.
	40 to 48 oz.	9-11 min.	Use 2-qt. covered casserole.
Exceptions: Tamales, Enchiladas	14½ to 15 oz.	3-5 min.	Do not remove paper wrappers from tamales. Arrange rolls in one layer in 1-qt. casserole. Cover.
Divider Pack Chow Mein	24 oz.	Sauce: 1-2 min. Veg: 1-2 min.	Follow photo directions, below. Use 1-qt. casserole.
	42 oz.	Sauce: 2-3 min. Veg: 1-3 min.	Follow photo directions, below. Use 1-qt. casserole.

Canned Main Dish Serving Suggestions:

- Chow Mein: Add canned or cooked chicken, tuna, shrimp, beef or pork; frozen peapods; or chopped green onions. Serve over chow mein noodles or rice, page 132.
- Tamales, Enchiladas: Top with dairy sour cream, shredded lettuce and cheese.
- Macaroni & Cheese: Add precooked sausage pieces or chopped, dried chives.
- Ravioli, Lasagna, Spaghetti: Sprinkle with grated Parmesan, shredded mozzarella or Cheddar cheese; stir in ¼ teaspoon dried basil leaves.
- Chili: Add drained, canned corn; 2 to 3 drops red pepper sauce; or 2 to 3 cups cooked, drained elbow macaroni.

How to Microwave Divider Pack Chow Mein

Empty small can of sauce into casserole; cover. Microwave at High as directed in chart, above, until hot and bubbly.

Drain and rinse the vegetables from the large can. Stir into sauce; cover.

Microwave at High as directed in chart until heated through. Stir before serving.

Canned Add-Meat Sauces

Canned add-meat sauces are combined with ground beef to make a main dish. You can also create your own add-meat combinations with cut-up leftover beef, pork or poultry. The additional time needed to heat sauce with leftovers will depend upon the amount of meat and the starting temperature of the meat.

How to Microwave Canned Add-Meat Sauces

Crumble ground beef into casserole as directed in Ground Beef Chart. Microwave at High until meat is no longer pink, stirring to break up pieces.

Drain. Stir in sauce of your choice. Microwave, uncovered, at High as directed in Add-Meat Sauce Chart, below, until hot, stirring after half the time.

Ground Beef Chart

Amt.	Casserole Size	Microwave Time at High
½ lb.	1½- to 2-qt.	2-3 min.
1 lb.	2-qt.	4-6 min.
2 lbs.	2-qt.	9-10 min.

Canned Add-Meat Sauce Chart

Item	Can Weight	Microwave Time at High	Procedure
Sloppy Joe Sauce			Follow photo directions, above.
	13 to 16 oz.	2-4 min.	Add sauce to 1 lb. browned ground beef as directed, above.
	27½ oz.	3-4 min.	Add sauce to 2 lbs. browned ground beef as directed, above.
Chili Sauce	27½ oz.	4-5 min.	Add sauce to ½ lb. browned ground beef as directed, above.

Canned Add-Meat Sauce Serving Suggestions:
• Sloppy Joes: Serve on bun spread with mustard, or on toasted English muffin. Sprinkle with shredded cheese.
• Chili: Serve topped with dairy sour cream, shredded cheese or crushed corn chips; or add 2 to 3 cups cooked elbow macaroni.

Canned Sauces & Gravies

Canned sauces and gravies are usually served over pasta, rice or potatoes as a side dish. You can use them to create a quick main dish with ground beef or leftover poultry by following the directions for add-meat sauces, page 108.

How to Microwave Canned Sauces & Gravies

Place contents of can in casserole as directed in chart. Cover with lid or plastic wrap.

Microwave at High as directed in chart until hot and bubbly. Small amounts with short heating times are stirred just before serving. Stir larger quantities after half the time and again before serving.

Canned Sauce & Gravy Chart

Item	Can Weight	Microwave Time at High	Procedure
Sauces Spaghetti, White, Mushroom, Pizza, Chili Dog			Follow photo directions, above.
	8 to 9 oz.	1-2 min.	Use 12- to 15-oz. bowl.
	10 to 16 oz.	3-4 min.	Use 1-qt. casserole.
	29 to 32 oz.	5-6 min.	Use 1- to 1½-qt. casserole.
	48 oz.	7-8 min.	Use 2-qt. casserole.
Gravies Beef, Brown, Pork, Chicken, Mushroom, Onion, Turkey			Follow photo directions, above.
	10 to 12 oz.	2-3½ min.	Use 1-qt. casserole or 15-oz. bowl.

Canned Vegetables

Canned vegetables are fully cooked and stored at room temperature, so microwaving time is based primarily upon quantity. Drain most of the liquid before heating; a minimum of moisture and a cover are sufficient to produce steam.

How to Microwave Canned Vegetables

Spoon 1 or 2 tablespoons of liquid from can into dish as directed in chart.

Drain vegetables. Add to dish. Cover with lid or plastic wrap.

Microwave at High as directed in chart until hot; stir after half the time and before serving.

Canned Vegetable Chart

Item	Can Weight	Microwave Time at High	Procedure
Whole, Slices & Cuts			Follow photo directions, above.
	7 to 9 oz.	1-2 min.	Reserve 1 tablespoon liquid. Use 12-oz. covered casserole or small serving bowl.
	14 to 20 oz.	2-3 min.	Reserve 2 tablespoons liquid. Use 1-qt. covered casserole.
	27 to 32 oz.	4-5 min.	Reserve 2 tablespoons liquid. Use 1-qt. covered casserole.

Canned Vegetable Serving Suggestions:
• Sprinkle with slivered almonds, chow mein noodles or French fried onions.

• Combine two kinds of canned vegetables.

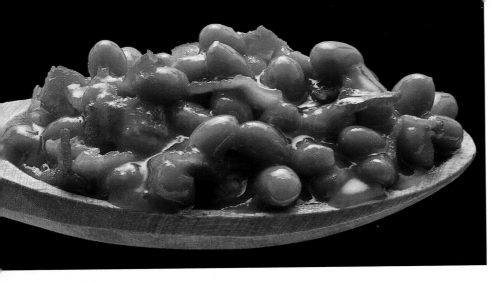

Canned Side Dishes

Canned side dishes are heated in the same manner as canned main dishes. They are heated from room temperature. The times in the chart are grouped by can weights.

How to Microwave Canned Side Dishes

Empty contents of can into bowl or casserole as directed in chart. Cover single servings with paper towel to prevent spatters. Cover larger amounts with casserole lid.

Microwave at High as directed in chart until heated, stirring after half the time.

Canned Side Dish Chart

Item	Can Weight	Microwave Time at High	Procedure
Side Dishes All except those listed below			Follow photo directions, above.
	7 to 8 oz.	1½-2½ min.	Use 15-oz. individual bowl.
	10½ to 16 oz.	2-5 min.	Use 1-qt. casserole.
	16 to 32 oz.	3-6 min.	Use 1-qt. casserole.
	40 oz.	6-7 min.	Use 2-qt. casserole.
	40 to 55 oz.	9-11 min.	Use 2-qt. casserole.
Exception: Wild Rice	14 oz.	2-4 min.	Rinse rice; drain. Place in 1-qt. covered casserole with 2 tablespoons water. Stir.

Canned Side Dish Serving Suggestions:
- Refried Beans: Top with sour cream, shredded Cheddar cheese or chopped onion.
- Baked Beans: Add cooked crumbled bacon, mustard, brown sugar, catsup or molasses.
- Wild Rice: Add canned mushrooms, drained; sliced water chestnuts; slivered, toasted almonds or chopped cooked celery.

Canned Soups

There are three types of canned soup. Condensed soups are diluted with a full can of water or milk. Add only half a soup can of liquid to semi-condensed soups. Ready-to-eat soups are not diluted at all. The type of liquid in the soup determines the power level used to microwave it. Ready-to-eat broth and soups diluted with water are heated at High. Use 50% (Medium) to microwave ready-to-eat cream soups and soups diluted with milk to prevent curdling.

Microwaving Techniques for Canned Soups

Select a 15-oz. bowl for single servings; no cover is needed. Place larger amounts in 1- to 1½-qt. covered casserole.

Microwave broth and water-based soups at High. Use 50% (Medium) for milk-based or cream soups.

Stir most soups after half the time and before serving. Soups diluted with water need not be stirred during cooking.

Canned Soup Chart

Item	Can Weight	Microwave Time	Procedure
Condensed Soups			Follow photo directions, above.
Water-Based	7½ to 13½ oz.	High: 2-3 min.	Use 1-qt. casserole with 1 can water.
Milk-Based	10½ to 15 oz.	50% (Medium): 6-12 min.	Use 1½-qt. casserole with 1 can milk.
Semi-Condensed Soups			Follow photo directions, above.
Water-Based	7¼ to 7¾ oz.	High: 1-3 min.	Use 15-oz. individual soup bowl with ½ can water.
	10½ to 10¾ oz.	High: 2-4 min.	Use 1-qt. casserole with ½ can water.
Milk-Based	11 oz.	50% (Medium): 6 min.	Use 1-qt. casserole with ½ can milk.
Ready-to-Serve Soups			Follow photo directions, above.
Broth Soups	7¼ to 7½ oz.	High: 1-2 min.	Use 15-oz. individual soup bowl.
	10 to 15 oz.	High: 2-4 min.	Use 15-oz. individual soup bowl.
	18¾ to 20 oz.	High: 3-5 min.	Use 1-qt. casserole.
Cream Soups	7¼ to 7½ oz.	50% (Medium): 3-4 min.	Use 15-oz. individual soup bowl.
	13 oz.	50% (Medium): 4-6 min.	Use 1-qt. casserole.

Canned Soup Serving Suggestions:

• Make New Soups From Two Soups, page 24.

• Garnish with pretzels, popcorn, seasoned croutons, crushed corn chips, shredded cheese or canned onion rings.

• Sprinkle with ½ to 1 teaspoon dried chives.

• Add chopped, cooked leftover meats or canned ham or chicken.

• Stir drained, canned mushrooms into beef or chicken broth soups.

• Blend in 1 to 2 teaspoons red or white wine.

Baby Food

Baby foods are warmed (80° to 90°F.), not heated. Check the label for manufacturer's heating precautions. Test the temperature before feeding the baby. The chart contains warming times for single-serving jars or half of the larger jars. Formula can also be warmed in the microwave oven.

How to Microwave Baby Formula

Do not use bottles with plastic liners; bags can melt. Use dishwasher-safe plastic or glass bottle. Microwave, without top, as directed in chart until warm. To test temperature, attach nipple and cap; shake bottle to redistribute heat. Sprinkle few drops on inner wrist.

Baby Food Chart

Item	Amount	Microwave Time at High: Room Temp.	Microwave Time at High: Refrigerated	Procedure
Baby Food Jars 3½ to 4¾ oz. or half of 7½ to 7¾ oz.	1 jar	15-30 sec.	30-40 sec.	Transfer food from jar into serving dish. Stir and check temperature after minimum time. Do not overheat. If necessary, continue microwaving. When microwaving 2 or more jars, check temperature after minimum time and remove any food that is warm.
	2 jars	30-40 sec.	1-1¼ min.	
	3 jars	40-60 sec.	1¼-1½ min.	
Baby Formula	4 oz.	15-20 sec.	25-40 sec.	Follow photo directions, above.
	6 oz.	20-30 sec.	30-45 sec.	
	8 oz.	30 sec.	45-60 sec.	

Dry Mixes

Dry mixes include main dishes, side dishes, sauces and desserts. Each section includes charts and step-by-step photo directions. In many dry mixes, less water is needed for microwaving than is called for in the conventional directions, so read the microwave instructions carefully.

Add-Meat Dinner Mixes

Most of these mixes are added to microwaved ground beef. Oriental-style mixes call for thinly sliced beef, pork or chicken. There are also several main dish mixes which use canned tuna.

Ground Beef Chart

Amount	Casserole Size	Microwave Time at High
½ lb.	1½- to 2-qt.	2 to 3 min.
1 lb.	2-qt.	4 to 6 min.

How to Microwave Ground Beef Dinner Mixes

Crumble ground beef into casserole. Microwave at High as directed in Ground Beef Chart, above, until meat is no longer pink, stirring after half the time to break apart pieces. Drain.

Add seasoning mix and other ingredients and microwave as directed in chart, page 118.

How to Microwave Stir-Fry Pepper Steak or Sukiyaki Dinner Mixes

Cut meat into thin strips as directed on package. Omit oil; place meat in 3-qt. casserole. Cover. Microwave at High 4 to 5 minutes, or until meat is no longer pink, stirring 2 or 3 times.

Blend sauce mix with water as directed on package. Add to meat. Microwave, uncovered, at High 3 to 5 minutes, or until boiling, stirring several times.

Drain and rinse vegetables. Stir into casserole. Microwave at High 2 minutes, or until heated through. Stir before serving.

How to Microwave Tuna Dinner Mixes

Reduce water by ½ cup. Measure into 2-qt. casserole. Drain 1 can (6½ oz.) tuna; place in casserole.

Add noodles and sauce mix. Cover. Microwave at High 10 minutes, stirring 3 times during cooking. Remove cover.

Microwave at High 4 to 5 minutes, or until noodles are tender and sauce thickens. Stir. Let stand 5 minutes.

How to Heat Tostada & Taco Shells

Heat tostada and taco shells by placing stack of shells on a paper towel. Microwave at High as directed in chart, right, until hot and slightly softened.

Shells	Microwave Time at High
2	15-20 seconds
4	25-30 seconds
6	30-45 seconds
8	45-60 seconds

Add-Meat Dinner Mix Chart

Item	Preparation	Microwave Instructions
Ground Beef Dinner Mix 6 to 8½ oz.	1. Follow photo directions, page 117. Use 1 lb. ground beef. 2. Reduce water by ½ cup. Stir water and remaining ingredients into ground beef. Cover.	1. Microwave at **High 10 minutes,** stirring 3 times. Remove cover. 2. Microwave at **High 5 minutes,** or until dry ingredients are tender. Let stand 5 minutes.
Tostada Mix 6¼ oz.	1. Follow photo directions, page 117. Use 1 lb. ground beef. 2. Reduce water by ¼ cup. Blend water and seasoning mix into ground beef.	1. Microwave at **High 8 to 10 minutes,** or until slightly thickened, stirring twice. 2. Heat tostada shells as directed, above. Spoon ⅓ cup meat mixture onto each shell.
Taco Mix 9¾ oz.	1. Follow photo directions, page 117. Use 1 lb. ground beef. 2. Reduce water by ½ cup. Blend water and seasoning mix into ground beef.	1. Microwave at **High 2 to 4 minutes,** or until slightly thickened. 2. Heat taco shells as directed, above. Fill with beef mixture. Garnish with shredded lettuce and cheese, if desired.

Item	Preparation	Microwave Instructions
Taco Casserole Mix 12½ oz.	1. Follow photo directions, page 117. Use 1 lb. ground beef. 2. Blend seasoning mix, tomato sauce and 1 cup hot water into ground beef.	1. Microwave at **High 8 to 9 minutes,** or until bubbly and thickened, stirring every 3 minutes. 2. Stir in taco chips. Let stand 2 minutes, or until chips soften.
Tamale Pie Mix 21¼ oz.	1. Follow photo directions, page 117. Use 1 lb. ground beef and 9-in. round baking dish. Add seasoning mix, sauce, corn and ¾ cup hot water. 2. Microwave at **High 5 to 8 minutes,** or until mixture is hot and bubbly. Sprinkle cornmeal over meat. Pour 1 cup hot water over cornmeal. Cover with plastic wrap.	1. Microwave at **High 3 minutes.** Remove plastic wrap. Rotate dish ¼ turn. 2. Microwave at **High 3 minutes,** or until cornmeal is set. Let stand 5 minutes.
Tuna Dinner Mix 7¾ to 8¾ oz.	1. Follow photo directions for Tuna Dinner Mixes, opposite.	
Tuna With Dumplings Dinner Mix 8 oz.	1. See photo directions for Tuna Dinner Mixes, opposite. Combine water, tuna, noodles and sauce mix as directed. Cover.	1. Microwave at **High 10 minutes.** Prepare dumplings as directed on package. Drop dumplings in 5 spoonfuls onto tuna mixture. Cover. 2. Microwave at **High 4 to 5 minutes,** or until dumplings are set and no longer doughy. Let stand, covered, 5 minutes.
Stir-Fry Pepper Steak or Sukiyaki Dinner Mix 29½ to 29¾ oz.	1. Use sirloin steak or round steak as directed on package.	1. Follow photo directions for Stir-Fry Pepper Steak or Sukiyaki Dinner Mixes, page 117.
Stir-Fry Chow Mein Dinner Mix 30 oz.	1. See photo directions for Stir-Fry Pepper Steak or Sukiyaki Dinner Mixes, page 117. Use chicken as directed on package.	1. Prepare meat as directed in photo directions, but blend drained and rinsed vegetables into meat along with the sauce. 2. Microwave at **High 6 to 9 minutes,** or until heated, stirring 2 or 3 times.
Sweet & Sour Dinner Mix 19 oz.	1. Cut 1 lb. lean pork into thin strips. Place in 2-qt. casserole; omit oil. Cover. 2. Microwave at **High 5 to 6 minutes,** or until meat is no longer pink, stirring twice. Drain. Add ¼ cup cold water and glaze mix.	1. Microwave at **High 2 to 4 minutes,** or until glaze boils and thickens, stirring twice. 2. Stir in sweet and sour sauce. Microwave at **High 1 to 2 minutes,** or until hot. Stir.

Sauce & Gravy Mixes

Sauce and gravy mixes are combined with either water or milk. Sauces can be microwaved at High because they are stirred after every minute with a wire whip. This prevents boil over and smooths the sauce.

How to Microwave Sauce & Gravy Mixes

Measure liquid as directed on package. Blend sauce mix and liquid in 2- or 4-cup measure.

Microwave at High as directed in chart, until sauce thickens or is hot and bubbly. Stir with wire whip after every minute.

Sauce & Gravy Mix Chart

Item	Preparation	Microwave Instructions
Water-Based Sauce & Gravy Mixes ¾ to 1¾ oz.	Follow photo directions, above.	If sauce contains ⅔ to 1 cup water, microwave at **High 1 to 3 minutes.** If sauce contains 1¼ cups water, microwave **3 to 5 minutes.**
Milk-Based Sauce & Gravy Mixes ¾ to 1¾ oz.	Follow photo directions, above. If butter is used, microwave in 1-qt. casserole at **High 1 to 2 minutes,** or until melted. Add sauce mix and milk as directed.	If sauce contains 1 cup milk, microwave at **High 2½ to 5 minutes.** If 1¼ cups milk is added, microwave **4 to 6 minutes;** microwave 2¼ cups milk **6 to 9 minutes.**
Exceptions: Spaghetti Sauce Mix 1½ to 2½ oz.	Use 1-qt. casserole. Measure liquid as directed on package. Add sauce mix and remaining ingredients as directed on package.	Microwave at **High 10 to 15 minutes,** or until hot and bubbly, stirring after every minute.
Béarnaise Sauce Mix ⅞ oz.	Melt ¼ cup butter in 4-cup measure at **High 1 to 1½ minutes.** Blend in liquid and sauce mix as directed.	Microwave at **High 3 to 4 minutes,** or until thickened, stirring after every minute.

Add-meat sauce and seasoning mixes are designed to give variety to ground beef, pork, beef and tuna. Special instructions are given in the chart, page 122, for meat loaf, meatballs and beef pieces. Since there is little evaporation during microwaving, some mixes require less water than conventional directions call for.

How to Microwave Ground Beef Sauce or Seasoning Mixes

Crumble 1 lb. ground beef into 2-qt. casserole. Microwave at High 4 to 6 minutes, or until meat is no longer pink, stirring to break up pieces. Drain.

Stir in sauce or seasoning mix and remaining ingredients as directed on package, reducing water if directed in the chart, page 122.

Microwave at High as directed in chart until flavors blend and mixture is hot and bubbly, stirring after half the time.

Add-Meat Sauce & Seasoning Mix Chart

Item	Preparation	Microwave Instructions
Beef Stew Seasoning Mix 1½ to 1¾ oz.	1. Coat 2 lbs. cubed stew meat with flour, if directed on package. Place in 3- to 5-qt. casserole. 2. Add 4 medium potatoes, quartered; 4 onions, quartered; 4 carrots, cut into 1-in. pieces; 4 stalks celery, cut into 1-in. pieces; and seasoning mix. Reduce water by 1 cup. Stir into beef.	1. Microwave, covered, at **High 5 minutes.** Stir. Reduce power to **50% (Medium).** 2. Microwave **1¼ to 1½ hours,** or until vegetables and meat are fork tender, stirring 3 or 4 times. Let stand, covered, 10 minutes.
Chili Seasoning Mix 1¼ to 1¾ oz.	1. Prepare 1 lb. ground beef in 2-qt. casserole as directed, page 121. 2. Add seasoning mix and remaining ingredients.	1. Microwave at **High 6 to 10 minutes,** or until flavors are blended and mixture is hot, stirring after half the time.
Chop Suey Sauce Mix 1⅝ oz.	1. Place 1 lb. cubed pork, beef or veal in 2-qt. casserole. 2. Microwave at **50% (Medium) 4 to 7 minutes,** or until meat is no longer pink. Drain. Add seasoning mix and 1 can (16 oz.) Chinese vegetables with liquid. Omit water.	1. Microwave at **High 4 to 6 minutes,** or until meat is tender and sauce is slightly thickened, stirring every 2 minutes.
Enchilada Sauce Mix 1⅛ to 1⅜ oz.	1. Combine seasoning mix and remaining ingredients in 1-qt. casserole. Blend in water. Microwave at **High 7 to 9 minutes,** or until mixture is thick and bubbly, stirring every 2 to 3 minutes. 2. Prepare ¾ to 1 lb. ground beef as directed, page 121. Drain.	1. Assemble enchiladas as directed on package, placing seam side down in 12 × 8-in. baking dish. 2. Microwave at **High 6 to 8 minutes,** or until cheese melts, rotating dish ½ turn after half the time. Let stand 5 minutes.
Meat Loaf Seasoning Mix 1⅛ to 3½ oz.	1. Prepare mix for 2 lbs. ground beef as directed on package. Pat mixture into ungreased 9 × 5-in. loaf dish.	1. Microwave at **High 15 to 20 minutes,** or until firm to touch and internal temperature is 145° to 155°, rotating dish ¼ turn every 5 minutes. Drain. Let stand 5 minutes.
Sloppy Joe or Pizza Sloppy Joe Seasoning Mix 1 to 1½ oz.	1. Prepare 1 lb. ground beef in 2-qt. casserole as directed, page 121. 2. Add seasoning mix and remaining ingredients.	1. Microwave at **High 3 to 6 minutes,** or until slightly thickened and flavors are blended, stirring after half the time.
Spaghetti Sauce Mix 1½ to 2½ oz.	1. Prepare ½ lb. ground beef in 2-qt. casserole as directed, page 121. 2. Add sauce mix and remaining ingredients.	1. Microwave at **High 10 to 20 minutes,** or until sauce is hot and bubbly.

Item	Preparation	Microwave Instructions
Stroganoff Seasoning Mix 1½ to 1¾ oz. With Meatballs	1. Shape 1 lb. ground beef into meatballs. Place in 2-qt. casserole. Microwave at **High 4 to 5 minutes,** or until meatballs are no longer pink, rearranging 2 or 3 times. Drain. Add seasoning mix and remaining ingredients.	1. Reduce power to **50% (Medium).** Microwave **10 to 15 minutes,** or until meat is tender and sauce is thick and bubbly, stirring every 5 minutes. Stir in sour cream, if directed. Serve over rice or noodles.
With Sirloin, Round, Chuck Steak or Tenderloin	1. Cut 1½ lbs. meat into 1-in. strips. Melt butter at **High 30 to 60 seconds.** Add meat; toss to coat. 2. Reduce power to **50% (Medium).** Microwave **10 to 15 minutes,** or until meat is no longer pink, stirring twice. Add seasoning mix and remaining ingredients.	1. Microwave at **50% (Medium) 10 to 15 minutes,** or until meat is tender and sauce is thick and bubbly, stirring every 5 minutes. Stir in sour cream, if directed. Serve over rice or noodles.
Sweet & Sour Sauce Mix 1¾ to 2 oz.	1. Cut 1 lb. lean pork into 1-in. cubes. Place in 2-qt. casserole. Microwave at **50% (Medium) 4 to 7 minutes,** or until meat is no longer pink. Drain. 2. Add seasoning mix and water as directed on package.	1. Microwave at **High 4 to 6 minutes,** or until meat is tender and sauce is slightly thickened, stirring twice during cooking.
Swiss Steak Seasoning Mix 1 oz.	1. Cut 1½ lbs. round steak into serving pieces. Place in 12 × 8-in. baking dish or cooking bag. Add water and seasoning mix. For thick sauce, blend small amount of water into ¼ cup flour; add to sauce. 2. Cover dish or tie bag with string, leaving small space for steam to escape. Place bag in baking dish.	1. Microwave at **50% (Medium) 25 minutes.** Rotate dish ½ turn and turn pieces of meat over. 2. Microwave at **50% (Medium) 15 to 20 minutes,** or until meat is tender. Let stand, covered, 10 minutes before serving.
Taco Seasoning Mix 1¼ oz.	1. Prepare 1 lb. ground beef in 2-qt. casserole as directed, page 121. 2. Reduce water by ¼ cup. Add water and seasoning mix to beef.	1. Microwave at **High 4 to 6 minutes,** or until thickened and bubbly.
2½ oz.	1. Prepare 2 lbs. ground beef in 2-qt. casserole as directed, page 121. 2. Reduce water by ¼ cup. Add water and seasoning mix to beef.	1. Microwave at **High 6 to 10 minutes,** or until mixture is hot and of desired consistency, stirring 2 or 3 times during cooking.
Tuna Casserole Sauce Mix 1½ oz.	1. Cook 1 to 1½ cups noodles conventionally while microwaving sauce. 2. In 2-qt. casserole, melt 1 tablespoon butter at **High 30 to 45 seconds.** Add seasoning mix and milk.	1. Microwave at **High 5 to 7 minutes,** or until bubbly and thickened, stirring after 2 minutes and then after every minute. 2. Blend in 1 can (7 oz.) drained tuna and cooked noodles. Microwave at **High 1 to 2 minutes,** or until hot. Stir before serving.

Pizza Mixes

For microwaved pizza with a crisp, brown crust, use one of two special utensils — the microwave pizza stone or pizza browner. These utensils have a special coating on the bottom that attracts and retains microwave energy during preheating. Because they become very hot, use hot pads when removing them from the oven and protect counters with a heat resistant pad. For greater safety, let utensils cool in the oven after use. For care and cleaning, follow manufacturer's directions. See page 93 for a special discussion of pizza utensil use and care.

Pizza Mix Chart

Item	Preparation	Microwave Instructions
Thin Crust Pizza	1. Follow photo directions, below. Follow package directions for preparation of thin crust.	1. Microwave crust at **50% (Medium) 2½ to 3½ minutes.** Add toppings. Increase power to **High.** 2. Microwave **4 to 6 minutes.**
Thick Crust Pizza	1. Follow photo directions, below. Follow package directions for preparation of thick crust.	1. Microwave crust at **50% (Medium) 4½ to 7 minutes.** Add toppings. Increase power to **High.** 2. Microwave **5 to 6 minutes.**

Pizza Mix Serving Suggestions:
• Top with microwaved ground beef, page 117, shredded mozzarella cheese, mushrooms, olives, green pepper, onions, etc.

How to Microwave Pizza Mix

Prepare dough as directed on package. Cut sheet of wax paper to fit microwave pizza utensil; grease generously.

Spread dough on paper into 11-in. circle, using buttered fingers. Prick with fork. Let rest as directed on package.

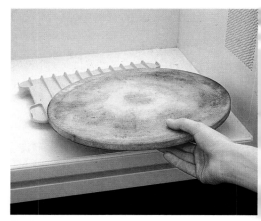

Preheat pizza browner at High 5 minutes or pizza stone set on roasting rack 7½ minutes.

Invert dough onto preheated stone or browner, being careful not to touch utensil with hands. Peel wax paper off dough.

Reduce power to 50% (Medium). Microwave as directed in chart, until crust is firm and no longer doughy.

Spread crust with sauce and cheese. Microwave at High as directed in chart, until center is hot and bubbly.

Meatless Dinner Mixes

Meatless dinner mixes include egg foo yung and noodle dinners. A noodle dinner is usually a meal by itself, but preparation techniques are similar to noodle side dish techniques, page 130. Checking the package will generally help you decide if your noodle mix is a dinner or a side dish.

Noodle dinners are prepared in a one- or two-step process. With the one-step noodle mixes, noodles and sauce are microwaved together. To prepare a two-step noodle mix, the noodles are microwaved first, drained and then combined with the sauce. The dinner is then microwaved briefly just to heat through. The dinners listed in the chart, page 128, are categorized by this cooking procedure.

How to Microwave Individual One-Step Noodle Dinner Mixes

Place contents of envelope in serving mug. Stir in hot tap water as directed on package.

Microwave at High 1 to 2 minutes, or until boiling.

Let stand, covered, 3 minutes. Stir before serving.

How to Microwave Two-Step Noodle Dinner Mixes

Measure 6 cups hot water into 3-qt. casserole. Add salt as directed. Cover with plastic wrap. Microwave at High 8 to 12 minutes, or until boiling.

Stir in noodles. Microwave, uncovered, at High 5 to 10 minutes, or until tender, stirring 3 times during cooking. Drain.

Mix in remaining ingredients as directed on package. Microwave at High 1 to 2 minutes, or until butter melts and noodles are hot. Stir.

Meatless Dinner Mix Chart

Item	Preparation	Microwave Instructions
Individual One-Step Noodle Dinner Mix Oriental, Italian, Beef or Cheese 2¾ to 4 oz.	1. Follow photo directions for Individual One-Step Noodle Dinner Mix, page 127. (Also pictured on page 116.)	
Two-Step Noodle Dinner Mix In Cheese, Beef, Chicken or Butter Sauce 8 oz.	1. Follow photo directions for Two-Step Noodle Dinner Mix, page 127.	
Macaroni & Cheese Dinner Mix 6 to 14½ oz.	1. Follow photo directions for Two-Step Noodle Dinner Mix, page 127.	
Spaghetti Dinner Mix 8 to 19½ oz.	1. Measure 6 cups hot water into 3-qt. casserole. Add salt as directed. Cover. Microwave at **High 8 to 12 minutes,** or until boiling. Add spaghetti. 2. Microwave at **High 6 to 10 minutes,** or until spaghetti is tender. Drain. Add butter, if directed. Serve with one of the following sauces, as directed on package.	1. **Prepared Sauce:** Pour sauce into 4-cup measure. Microwave at **High 3 to 4 minutes,** or until heated. Serve over spaghetti. **Sauce Mix:** Prepare by adding tomato paste or sauce, butter and water as directed on package. Microwave at **High 5 minutes,** or until heated, stirring after half the time. Serve over spaghetti.
Egg Foo Yung Mix 30¼ oz.	1. Combine patty ingredients as directed on package. Preheat browning dish at **High 5 minutes.** 2. Coat dish with 1 tablespoon vegetable oil. Ladle 3 patties (⅓ cup each) onto dish, spreading vegetables evenly. 3. Reduce power to **70% (Medium-High).**	1. Microwave patties **3 to 5 minutes,** or until set, turning over after half the time. Remove from dish. 2. Reheat dish at **High 2 minutes** between each batch. Repeat with remaining patties. 3. In 4-cup measure combine sauce mix and hot water as directed on package. Microwave at **High 4 to 6 minutes,** or until thickened, stirring after 2 minutes, then every minute. Serve over patties.

Meatless Dinner Mix Serving Suggestions:

• Serve egg foo yung with Fried Rice, page 42.

• Serve noodle casseroles with one of the topping suggestions, page 61.

• Add precooked sausage to macaroni & cheese.

Side Dish Mixes

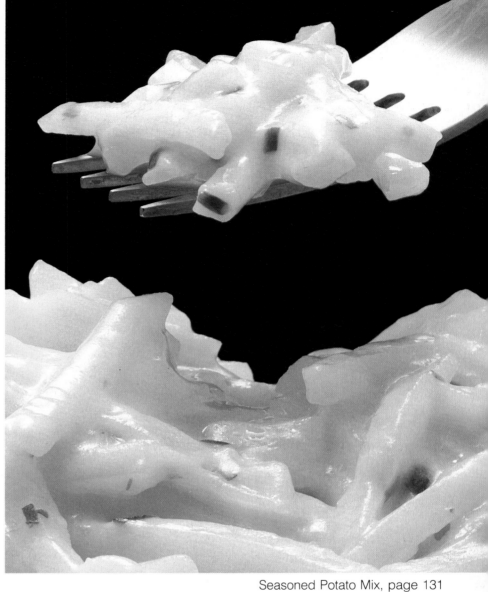

Side dish mixes include potato casseroles, instant mashed potatoes, bread stuffing mixes, and noodle side dishes.

Since there is little evaporation during microwaving, some of these mixes require less water than the conventional directions call for. Carefully read the chart, page 131, for water amounts.

Noodle side dishes are prepared in two ways. With a one-step mix, noodles and sauce are microwaved together. For a two-step mix, microwave and drain the noodles before combining them with sauce.

Seasoned Potato Mix, page 131

How to Microwave Instant Mashed Potatoes

Combine butter, water, salt and milk as directed on package, using casserole recommended in chart, page 131. Cover.

Microwave at High until boiling, following times given in chart for number of servings desired. Stir in potato flakes.

Stir potatoes until they are of desired consistency.

Stuffing Mix, page 131

How to Microwave One-Step Noodle Side Dish Mixes

Reduce water by ¼ cup. Pour into 2-qt. casserole with sauce mix and noodles. Stir; cover.

Microwave at High 5 minutes. Stir. Microwave, uncovered, 5 to 6 minutes, or until noodles are tender and sauce thickens.

Let stand, covered, 5 minutes. Stir in butter, if directed.

How to Microwave Two-Step Noodle Side Dish Mixes

Measure 6 cups water into 3-qt. casserole. Add salt as directed. Cover. Microwave at High 8 to 12 minutes, or until boiling.

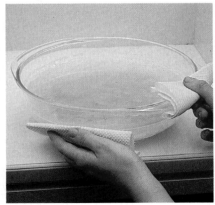

Stir in noodles. Microwave, uncovered, at High 5 to 10 minutes, or until noodles are tender, stirring 3 times. Drain.

Add milk, butter and seasonings as directed on package. Stir. Microwave at High 1 to 2 minutes, or until heated.

Side Dish Mix Chart

Item	Preparation	Microwave Instructions
One-Step Noodle Side Dish Mix In Beef, Chicken, Cheese, or Butter Sauce 4¼ to 4½ oz.	1. Follow photo directions for One-Step Noodle Side Dish Mix, opposite.	
Two-Step Noodle Side Dish Mix Parmesan, Almondine, Stroganoff, Romanoff 5¼ to 7¼ oz.	1. Follow photo directions for Two-Step Noodle Side Dish Mix, opposite.	
Seasoned Potato Mix 4¾ to 5⅝ oz.	1. Place butter in 2-qt. casserole. Microwave at **High 30 to 60 seconds,** or until melted. 2. Reduce water by ½ cup. Add water, potatoes, seasonings and milk to casserole; cover.	1. Microwave at **High 5 minutes.** Stir. 2. Microwave, uncovered, at **High 7 to 10 minutes,** or until potatoes are tender and sauce thickens, stirring twice. Let stand, uncovered, 5 minutes. Stir before serving.
11 oz.	1. Place butter in 3-qt. casserole. Microwave at **High 1½ to 2 minutes,** or until melted. 2. Reduce water by 1 cup. Add water, potatoes, seasonings and milk to casserole; cover.	1. Microwave at **High 8 to 10 minutes,** stirring once. 2. Microwave, uncovered, at **High 10 to 15 minutes,** or until potatoes are tender and sauce thickens, stirring every 5 minutes. Let stand, uncovered, 5 minutes. Stir before serving.

Instant Mashed Potato Mix
 30 to 48 oz.
	1. Follow photo directions, page 129, using 1-qt. casserole for 2 and 4 servings or 2-qt. casserole for 6 servings.	1. Microwave at **High.**
		  2 servings: **2 to 3 minutes**
		  4 servings: **3 to 4 minutes**
		  6 servings: **5 to 7 minutes**

Stuffing Mix 6 to 6½ oz.	1. Combine water, butter and stuffing mix in 2-qt. casserole as directed on package. Cover.	1. Microwave bread stuffing mix at **High 4 to 6 minutes,** or until fully rehydrated, stirring once. Microwave stuffing with rice at **High 6 to 8 minutes.** 2. Let stand, covered, 5 minutes, until liquid is absorbed.
Spaetzle Mix 10 oz.	1. Measure 6 cups water into 3-qt. casserole. Add salt as directed on package. Cover. 2. Microwave at **High 8 to 12 minutes,** or until boiling. Stir in spaetzle.	1. Microwave, uncovered, at **High 9 to 10 minutes,** or until spaetzle are tender. 2. Let stand, covered, 10 minutes. Drain. Serve as directed on package.

Rice & Rice Mixes

Rice and rice mixes microwave well. Because the energy penetrates the dish from all sides there is little danger of scorching the rice. Prepare rice in a serving dish and save on clean-up time.

Use the photo directions below for all rice and rice mixes except instant rice. To determine which microwave instructions apply to your rice mix, check the conventional cooking time on your package. The chart, opposite, is organized by conventional cooking times.

Follow the package directions for ingredient measurements and use the chart for the microwave procedures and cooking times. Standing time is important because it allows the rice to absorb all the liquid.

How to Microwave Rice & Rice Mixes

Measure hot water, butter, rice and seasonings into 2-qt. casserole as directed on package. Cover.

Microwave at High as directed in chart until boiling. Stir. Reduce power to 50% (Medium). Microwave until rice is tender, stirring 2 or 3 times.

Let stand, covered, until all liquid is absorbed. Fluff with fork before serving.

Rice & Rice Mix Chart

Item	Preparation	Microwave Instructions
Instant Rice	1. Measure hot water, butter, salt and seasonings into 1- to 2-qt. casserole as directed on package. Cover.	1. Microwave at **High** until boiling. 2 servings: **2 to 3 minutes** 4 servings: **3 to 4 minutes** 6 servings: **5 to 7 minutes** 2. Stir in rice. Cover. Let stand 5 minutes, or until rice is tender Fluff with fork before serving.
5 Minute Seasoned Rice Mix	1. Follow photo directions, opposite.	1. Microwave at **High 4 to 5 minutes.** 2. Microwave at **50% (Medium) 3 to 4 minutes.** 3. Let stand 10 minutes.
10 to 15 Minute Seasoned Rice Mix	1. If package contains rice and vermicelli mixture, mix with butter in 2-qt. casserole. Microwave at **High 3 to 4 minutes,** or until mixture is golden brown, stirring after half the time. 2. Add remaining ingredients, following photo directions, opposite.	1. Microwave at **High 4 to 6 minutes.** 2. Microwave at **50% (Medium) 5 to 10 minutes.** 3. Let stand 10 to 15 minutes.
20 to 30 Minute Seasoned Rice Mix	1. If package contains rice and vermicelli mixture, mix with butter in 2-qt. casserole. Microwave at **High 3 to 4 minutes,** or until mixture is golden brown, stirring after half the time. 2. Add remaining ingredients, following photo directions, opposite.	1. Microwave at **High 5 to 7 minutes.** 2. Microwave at **50% (Medium) 10 to 20 minutes.** 3. Let stand 10 to 15 minutes.
40 to 60 Minute Seasoned Rice Mix	1. Follow photo directions, opposite.	1. Microwave at **High 6 to 8 minutes.** 2. Microwave at **50% (Medium) 20 to 30 minutes.** 3. Let stand 10 to 15 minutes.
Long Grain Rice	1. Follow photo directions, opposite. ½ cup rice: 1- to 1½-qt. casserole 1 cup rice: 2-qt. casserole	1. Microwave at **High.** ½ cup rice: **3 minutes** 1 cup rice: **5 minutes** 2. Microwave at **50% (Medium).** ½ cup rice: **8 to 10 minutes** 1 cup rice: **11 to 15 minutes** 3. Let stand 2 to 4 minutes.
Rice in Pouch	1. Measure 4 cups salted water into 2-qt. casserole. Cover.	1. Microwave at **High 6 to 8 minutes,** or until boiling. 2. Drop one pouch into boiling water. Microwave, uncovered, at **High 15 minutes.** Drain. Empty rice into dish and fluff with fork.

Cereals

Individual servings of instant cereal can be prepared right in the serving bowl. For cooked cereals, such as oatmeal, creamed wheat and grits, choose a container large enough to prevent boil over. Since personal tastes differ, total microwaving time will depend upon the cereal consistency you prefer.

How to Microwave Cereals

Measure cereal and salt as directed on package. Place in casserole recommended in chart, below. Stir in hot water as directed.

Microwave at High for half the minimum time. Stir. Microwave remaining time, or until cereal reaches desired thickness, stirring 2 or 3 times during cooking. Stir before serving.

Cereal Chart

Item	Preparation	Microwave Instructions
Regular Cereal 14 to 42 oz.	1. Follow photo directions, above, using the following casseroles: 1 serving: 1-qt. casserole 2 servings: 2-qt. casserole 4 servings: 3-qt. casserole	1. Microwave at **High,** until cereal reaches desired thickness. 1 serving: **3 to 4 minutes** 2 servings: **5 to 6 minutes** 4 servings: **7 to 8 minutes**
Quick-Cooking Cereal 14 to 42 oz.	1. Follow photo directions, above, using the following casseroles: 1 serving: 1-qt. casserole 2 servings: 2-qt. casserole 4 servings: 3-qt. casserole	1. Microwave at **High** until cereal reaches desired thickness. 1 serving: **2 to 3 minutes** 2 servings: **3 to 4 minutes** 4 servings: **6 to 7 minutes**
Individual Instant Cereal 10 to 12 oz.	1. Measure ½ cup hot water into 1-cup measure.	1. Microwave at **High 1 to 2 minutes,** or until boiling. 2. Empty 1 envelope into serving bowl. Pour in boiling water. Stir. Let stand 1 to 2 minutes.
Baby Food Cereal 8 oz.	1. Place 4 to 5 tablespoons milk or baby formula in small dish or 1-cup measure.	1. Microwave at **High 20 to 30 seconds,** or until warm. 2. Stir in 1 tablespoon cereal.

Cereal Serving Suggestions:
• Stir in raisins, chopped dates, dried apples, brown sugar, butter or cinnamon and sugar.

Beverage & Soup Mixes

Beverage mixes include hot chocolate, tea and instant coffee. They are mixed with either water or milk.

Soup mixes come in several forms, from instant single servings to family-size packets. Some include packets of quick-cooking noodles and dehyrated vegetables. Others call for additional ingredients, such as meat.

Beverage & Soup Mix Chart

Item	Preparation	Microwave Instructions
Beverage Mix Hot Chocolate, Tea, Instant Coffee	Pour ¾ cup hot water or 1 cup milk into 1- to 2-cup measure.	Microwave at **High** until boiling. ¾ cup water: **1½ to 2 minutes** 1 cup milk: **2 to 3 minutes** Combine liquid and beverage mix as directed on package.
Individual Instant Soup Mix 1 to 3½ oz. box (4 envelopes)	Pour ¾ cup hot water into 1-cup measure.	Microwave at **High 1½ to 2 minutes,** or until boiling. Pour contents of 1 envelope into serving dish. Stir in boiling water until mix dissolves.
Instant Bouillon Mix 2 to 6½ oz.	Measure hot water as directed on package into 1-cup measure or serving mug.	Microwave at **High 2 to 3 minutes,** or until boiling. Stir in bouillon until dissolved.
Oriental Noodle Soup Mix 1½ to 3½ oz.	Measure hot water into 1-qt. casserole as directed on package. Cover. Microwave at **High 3 to 4 minutes,** or until boiling. Add noodles. Cover.	Microwave at **High 3 minutes,** or until noodles are tender, stirring once during cooking. Stir in soup mix until dissolved.
Instant Soup Mix 2 to 4¼ oz.	Place contents of envelope in 2-qt. casserole. Stir in hot water as directed on package. Cover.	Microwave at **High 4 to 10 minutes,** or until vegetables are rehydrated, stirring once during cooking.
Add-Meat Soup Mix 6½ to 9½ oz.	Combine meat recommended on package with water and soup mix in 5-qt. casserole; cover.	Microwave at **High 10 minutes.** Microwave at **50% (Medium) 50 to 60 minutes,** or until meat and vegetables are tender, stirring 3 or 4 times.

Quick Bread Mixes

To give quick bread crusts a golden-brown color, grease the loaf dish and coat with graham cracker crumbs. Quick breads which are served from the baking dish need no special dish preparation. Toppings are generally sprinkled on coffee cakes part way through microwaving. They may sink into the batter if they are added before microwaving.

To help square and loaf-shaped breads microwave evenly, place them on an inverted saucer and shield the corners or ends with foil for part of the cooking time.

Quick breads are started at 50% (Medium) and finished at High, with the exception of muffins, which are microwaved at High. Let bread stand directly on counter to complete cooking and allow moist spots to dry. Cool muffins on wire rack.

How to Microwave Quick Bread Mixes

Grease 8 × 5-in. loaf dish. If batter is light-colored, coat bottom and sides with graham cracker crumbs or sugar. Prepare batter as directed on package; pour into dish.

Shield ends of dishes if directed in chart, page 138, to prevent overcooking. Shield loaf dish with 2-in. wide strips of foil, covering 1 inch of batter and molding remainder around handles. Use triangles of foil in corners of square dish. Quick breads baked in round dishes need no shielding.

Place dish on inverted saucer in oven. Microwave at 50% (Medium), rotating as directed in chart, page 138.

Remove shields. Increase power to High. Microwave remaining time or until center springs back when lightly touched. A wooden pick inserted in center should come out clean and no uncooked batter should appear through bottom of dish. Let dish stand directly on counter 3 to 5 minutes. To serve loaves, loosen edges; invert onto rack. Cool. Serve other quick breads warm from dish.

Quick Bread Mix Chart

Item	Preparation	Microwave Instructions
Quick Bread Mix 15 to 17 oz.	1. Follow photo directions, page 137, using 8 × 5-in. loaf dish. Shield ends of dish.	1. Microwave at **50% (Medium) 9 minutes,** rotating ¼ turn every 3 minutes. Remove shields. Increase power to **High.** 2. Microwave **2 to 8 minutes,** or until center tests done, rotating every 2 minutes.
Corn Bread Mix 15 oz.	1. Follow photo directions, page 137, using 8 × 8-in. baking dish. Shield corners of dish with foil triangles.	1. Microwave at **50% (Medium) 5 minutes,** rotating after half the time. Increase power to **High.** 2. Microwave **2 to 5 minutes,** or until center tests done, rotating after half the time.
Gingerbread Mix 14 to 14½ oz.	1. Prepare batter as directed on package. Pour into 8 × 8-in. baking dish. Do not shield.	1. Microwave at **50% (Medium) 6 minutes,** rotating after half the time. Increase power to **High.** 2. Microwave **3 to 6 minutes,** or until center tests done, rotating 2 or 3 times.
Coffee Cake Mix 10½ oz.	1. Prepare batter as directed on package. Pour into 9-in. round cake dish. Sprinkle with topping.	1. Microwave at **50% (Medium) 3 minutes.** Rotate dish. Increase power to **High.** 2. Microwave **1 to 4 minutes,** or until center tests done, rotating every 2 minutes.
14 to 19 oz.	1. For cooked topping, prepare topping mix as directed on package. Microwave at **High 1 to 2 minutes,** or until boiling, stirring once. Reduce power to **50% (Medium).** Microwave **1 minute,** stirring once. Set aside. 2. Prepare coffee cake batter as directed on package. Assemble coffee cake in 9-in. round cake dish as directed on package; reserve final topping layer.	1. Microwave at **50% (Medium) 6 minutes,** rotating after half the time. Sprinkle with final layer of topping, or drizzle cooked topping over cake. Increase power to **High.** 2. Microwave **1 to 4 minutes,** or until cake springs back when lightly touched, rotating every 2 minutes.
Muffin Mix 7 to 13 oz.	1. Prepare batter as directed on package. Line microwave muffin cups or custard cups with 2 paper baking cups. 2. Fill each cup half full. Arrange muffins in ring in oven.	1. Microwave at **High** until dry on top, rotating once. 1 muffin: **½ to ¾ minute** 2 muffins: **1 to 1½ minutes** 4 muffins: **1½ to 2½ minutes** 6 muffins: **2½ to 4½ minutes** 2. Remove immediately to wire rack to cool.

Cake mixes rise higher in a microwave oven than they do when baked conventionally, so be sure to use the baking dish recommended and fill only half full. Extra batter can be used to prepare cupcakes. Elevating the cake on an inverted saucer and starting at 50% (Medium) promotes even baking. After cake tests done, let stand directly on counter; trapped heat completes cooking. If a few moist spots appear on top, they will dry as cake cools.

How to Microwave Cake Mixes

Prepare mix as directed on package. Prepare baking dish recommended in chart, below.

Place dish on inverted saucer. Microwave at 50% (Medium) for first part of time, rotating and shielding as directed in chart. Increase power to High.

Microwave remaining time, or until top springs back and wooden pick inserted in center comes out clean. Let stand directly on counter 10 minutes.

How to Microwave Ring Cake Mixes

Grease ring dish. Coat with fine graham cracker crumbs or sugar. Prepare mix as directed on package; pour into dish. Set on inverted saucer in oven.

Microwave at 50% (Medium) as directed in chart. Increase power to High. Microwave until top springs back and no unbaked batter appears.

Let stand directly on counter 10 to 15 minutes. Loosen edges and invert cake onto plate. Cool completely before frosting.

Cake Mix Chart

Item	Preparation	Microwave Instructions
One-Layer Cake Mix 9 oz.	1. Follow photo directions for cake mixes, above. Use 9-in. round dish lined with wax paper or 8 × 8-in. square baking dish.	1. Microwave at **50% (Medium) 6 minutes.** 2. Increase power to **High.** Microwave **2 to 5 minutes.**
Two-Layer Cake Mix 18 to 20 oz. Two layers	1. Follow photo directions for cake mixes, above. Use two 9-in. round dishes lined with wax paper or two 8 × 8-in. square dishes.	1. Microwave one layer at a time following instructions for One-Layer Cake Mix, above.
Rectangle plus cupcakes	1. Follow photo directions for cake mixes, above. Reserve ⅔ cup batter. Pour remaining batter into 12 × 8-in. baking dish. Shield ends with 3-in. wide strips of foil. 2. Use reserved batter to prepare cupcakes. Follow directions for Muffin Mix, page 138.	1. Microwave cake at **50% (Medium) 9 minutes,** rotating ½ turn every 3 minutes. Remove foil. 2. Increase power to **High.** Microwave **2 to 7 minutes.**

Item	Preparation	Microwave Instructions
Cake Mix & Frosting 11 to 13½ oz.	1. Follow photo directions for cake mixes, opposite. Use paperboard container provided in package.	1. Microwave at **50% (Medium) 3 minutes.** Rotate ¼ turn. 2. Increase power to **High.** Microwave **1 to 4 minutes,** rotating every 2 minutes. 3. Frost cooled cake with frosting envelope provided in package.
Snack Cake Mix 13½ to 14 oz.	1. Follow photo directions for cake mixes, opposite. Use 8 × 8-in. baking dish.	1. Microwave at **50% (Medium) 5 minutes,** rotating after half the time. Shield corners with foil. 2. Increase power to **High.** Microwave **2 to 5 minutes.**
Ring Cake Mix 22½ to 27 oz.	1. Follow photo directions for ring cakes, opposite. Use 12- or 14-cup ring baking dish.	1. Microwave at **50% (Medium) 12 minutes,** rotating every 3 minutes. 2. Increase power to **High.** Microwave **2 to 7 minutes,** rotating every 2 minutes.
Pound Cake Mix 16 to 17 oz.	1. Follow photo directions for ring cakes, opposite. Use 8- or 12-cup ring baking dish.	1. Microwave at **50% (Medium) 8 minutes,** rotating every 3 minutes. 2. Increase power to **High.** Microwave **1 to 4 minutes,** rotating after each minute.
Boston Cream Pie Mix 15½ oz.	1. Follow photo directions for cake mixes, opposite. 2. Use 9-in. round baking dish lined with wax paper.	1. Microwave at **50% (Medium) 6 minutes,** rotating after 3 minutes. 2. Increase power to **High.** Microwave **1 to 2 minutes.** 3. Let stand 5 minutes. Invert onto serving plate to cool. Prepare filling and glaze; assemble as directed on package.
Pineapple Upside-Down Cake Mix 21½ oz.	1. Microwave 2 tablespoons butter in 8 × 8-in. baking dish at **High 30 to 60 seconds,** or until melted. Sprinkle with topping mix and fruit as directed on package. 2. Prepare cake mix as directed on package; pour over topping in dish. Place on inverted saucer in oven.	1. Microwave at **50% (Medium) 6 minutes,** rotating after 3 minutes. 2. Increase power to **High.** Microwave **4 to 7 minutes,** or until center springs back when lightly touched, rotating twice. 3. Let cake stand on counter 5 minutes. Invert onto serving plate.

Cake Mix Serving Suggestions:

- Frost with canned or box mix frostings.
- Sprinkle with toasted coconut.
- Sprinkle with decorative candies.

- Serve with dessert sauces or ice cream toppings, page 61.
- Sprinkle cooled cake with powdered sugar.

Cookie, Bar & Brownie Mixes

A porous microwave pizza stone can be used for microwaving cookies. However, the pizza browner is not satisfactory because it does not absorb moisture. See page 93 for detailed instructions on using the pizza stone.

Basic brownies are made from a dense batter which microwaves best at 50% (Medium). When increasing power to High for cake-like brownies and other bars, shield corners of dish to prevent overcooking.

How to Microwave Cookie Mixes

Prepare cookie dough as directed on package. Place pizza stone on roasting rack. Preheat at High 5 minutes. Do not use pizza browner.

Drop 8 teaspoons of dough around edge of stone. Microwave at High 1 to 5 minutes, or until cookies are no longer doughy, rotating stone every minute.

Remove cookies to cooling rack. Preheat stone at High 3 minutes between each batch. Repeat with remaining dough.

Cookie & Bar Mix Chart

Item	Preparation	Microwave Instructions
Cookie Mix 15 to 16 oz.	1. Follow photo directions, above.	
Date Bar Mix 14 oz.	1. Use 8 × 8-in. glass baking dish. Prepare date mix and crumb mix as directed on package. Press half of crumb mixture into dish. 2. Pour date mixture over crumbs. Sprinkle with remaining crumbs; press lightly.	1. Shield corners of dish with foil triangles. Place on inverted saucer in oven. 2. Microwave at **High 5 to 8 minutes,** or until center is hot and slightly firm to the touch, rotating every 2 minutes.

How to Microwave Basic Brownies

Prepare batter for conventional brownies as directed on package. Spread in baking dish recommended in chart, below.

Place dish on inverted saucer. Microwave at 50% (Medium) as directed in chart, below, rotating every 2 to 3 minutes.

Insert knife in center. It should come out clean, and brownies should be dry on bottom. Let cool completely before cutting.

How to Microwave Cake-Like Brownies

Prepare batter for conventional cake-like brownies as directed on package. Spread in baking dish recommended in chart, below. Place on inverted saucer.

Microwave at 50% (Medium) as directed in chart, below, rotating once. Shield corners of dish with foil. Increase power to High. Microwave as directed.

Look through bottom of dish. No unbaked batter should appear. Center top springs back when lightly touched. Let cool completely.

Brownie Mix Chart

Item	Preparation	Microwave Instructions
Basic Brownies 15 to 16 oz.	Follow photo directions, above. Use ungreased 8 × 8-in. or 9 × 9-in. glass baking dish.	Microwave at **50% (Medium) 10 to 15 minutes,** rotating dish every 2 to 3 minutes.
21½ to 23½ oz.	Follow photo directions, above. Use two ungreased 8 × 8-in. or 9 × 9-in. glass baking dishes.	Microwave one dish at a time at **50% (Medium) 10 to 15 minutes,** rotating dish every 2 to 3 minutes.
Cake-Like Brownies 15 to 16 oz.	Follow photo directions, above. Use ungreased 8 × 8-in. or 9 × 9-in. glass baking dish.	Microwave at **50% (Medium) 6 minutes,** rotating once. Shield. Increase power to **High.** Microwave **2 to 6 minutes.**
21½ to 23½ oz.	Follow photo directions, above. Use two ungreased 8 × 8-in. or 9 × 9-in. glass baking dishes.	Microwave one dish at a time at **50% (Medium) 6 minutes,** rotating once. Shield. Increase power to **High.** Microwave **2 to 6 minutes.**

Brownie Mix Serving Suggestions:
• Frost cooled brownies; sprinkle with chopped nuts or chopped maraschino cherries.

Pie Crust Mixes

Pie crusts are microwaved before filling because uncooked pastry absorbs moisture from the filling. For a double crust look, cut out pastry shapes, microwave on wax paper at High 2 to 4 minutes, or until dry and opaque. Arrange cut-outs on top of prepared pie.

How to Microwave Pie Crust Mix & Sticks

Prepare dough as directed on package, adding 3 or 4 drops yellow food coloring to water before mixing. Roll out to ⅛-in. thick circle at least 2 inches larger than inverted pie plate. Fit into pie plate.

Finish edges and prick generously. Microwave at High as directed in chart, below, rotating ½ turn every 2 minutes. Shield any brown spots with pieces of foil. If crust bubbles, gently push down.

Watch closely; check for doneness before minimum time by looking through bottom of plate. Crust will not brown, but will appear dry and opaque.

How to Microwave Graham Cracker Crust

Measure ¼ cup plus 1 tablespoon butter or margarine into 9- or 10-in. pie plate. Microwave at High 45 to 60 seconds, or until melted.

Stir in 1⅓ cups fine graham cracker crumbs and 2 tablespoons brown or granulated sugar. Reserve 2 tablespoons crumb mixture for garnish.

Press remaining crumbs firmly against bottom and sides of plate. Microwave at High as directed in chart, below, rotating ½ turn after 1 minute. Cool; fill.

Pie Crust Mix Chart

Item	Preparation	Microwave Instructions
Pie Crust Mix & Sticks 11 to 22 oz.	Follow photo directions for Pie Crust Mix & Sticks, above. If adding sweet filling, such as fruit pie filling, brush crust lightly with vanilla to give a richer color.	Microwave at **High 5 to 7 minutes**, rotating twice. If adding liquid filling, brush microwaved crust with slightly beaten egg yolk. Microwave at High 30 to 60 seconds or until set.
Graham Cracker Crust 13½ oz.	Follow photo directions for Graham Cracker Crust, above.	Microwave at **High 1½ minutes.**

Pudding, Pie Filling & Gelatin Mixes

Pudding and pie filling mixes are easily prepared in the microwave. A little stirring with a wire whip keeps them smooth. To prevent skin formation during cooling, place plastic wrap directly on the pudding surface.

How to Microwave Pudding & Pie Filling Mixes

Place pudding mix in casserole or 4-cup measure. Blend in milk and remaining ingredients as directed on package.

Microwave at High as directed in chart, below, stirring with wire whip after the first time. Microwave remaining time until boiling or thickened as directed on package, stirring each minute.

Cool as directed on package. Pour into serving dishes or microwaved pie crust. Mixture thickens as it stands. Chill.

Pudding, Pie Filling & Gelatin Mix Chart

Item	Preparation	Microwave Instructions
Pudding & Pie Filling Mixes 1½ to 4⅛ oz.	Follow photo directions, above, using 4-cup measure or 1½-qt. casserole.	Microwave at **High 2 minutes. Stir.** Microwave **4 to 6 minutes.**
4½ to 6⅛ oz.	Follow photo directions, above, using 2-qt. casserole.	Microwave at **High 3 minutes. Stir.** Microwave **4 to 5 minutes.**
Gelatin Mixes ⅝ to 6 oz.	Follow package directions for amount of water. Pour into 4-cup measure.	Microwave 1 cup hot water at **High 2 to 3 minutes,** or 2 cups **3 to 5 minutes,** until boiling. Stir into gelatin until dissolved. Add cold water as directed on package. Pour into serving dishes. Chill until set.

Refrigerated Foods

The dairy case and meat cooler of your supermarket offer a number of foods which are convenient to use by themselves, or combine with other ingredients when speed and ease of preparation are important. In addition to the foods listed in these charts, sliced or grated cheese and prepared cheese spreads add variety to convenience cooking.

Refrigerated Rolls Chart

Item	Amount	Microwave Time	Procedure
Refrigerated Sweet Rolls 9½ to 11 oz.	7 to 9 rolls	50% (Med.): 5-8 min.	Arrange rolls in 9-in. pie plate. Place on inverted saucer in oven. Microwave until springy to touch, rotating ¼ turn every 2 minutes. Frost and serve hot.
Refrigerated Prebaked Buttermilk or Baking Powder Biscuits 11 oz.	2 biscuits 4 biscuits 6 biscuits	High: 20-25 sec. High: 30-45 sec. High: ¾-1¼ min.	Place biscuits on paper towel-lined serving dish. Microwave until warm to touch, rotating after half the time.

Softening Butter & Cream Cheese Chart

Item	Amount	Microwave Time	Procedure
Cream Cheese	3 oz. 8 oz.	50% (Med.): ½-1 min. 50% (Med.): 1-1½ min.	Place cheese in dish. Microwave until just softened.
Butter or Margarine	½ cup (1 stick)	30% (Low): 10-50 sec.	Place butter in serving dish. Check frequently. Microwave until just softened.

How to Microwave Sausage Patties or Links

Preheat browning dish at High 5 minutes. Place sausages or links in dish.

Microwave first side at High as directed in chart, below. Turn sausages over.

Microwave second side at High until center of sausage is firm to the touch.

Sausage Patty & Link Chart

Item	Amount	Microwave Time at High: 1st side	Microwave Time at High: 2nd side	Procedure
Fresh Bulk Pork Sausage 12 to 16 oz. ½-in. slices	2 4 8	½ min. 1½ min. 2 min.	1 min. 1½-2 min. 2½-3 min.	Follow photo directions, above. If sausage is frozen, defrost as directed, page 104.
Fresh Pork Sausage Links	2 4 8	½ min. ½-1 min. 1-1½ min.	½-1 min. 1 min. 1½ min.	Follow photo directions, above.
Precooked Pork Sausage Links	2 4 8	¼ min. ½ min. ½ min.	¼-½ min. ½ min. ½-¾ min.	Follow photo directions, above.
Canned Patties Sausage, Ham, Ham & Cheese 12 to 36 oz.	6	1 min.	1-1½ min.	Follow photo directions, above.

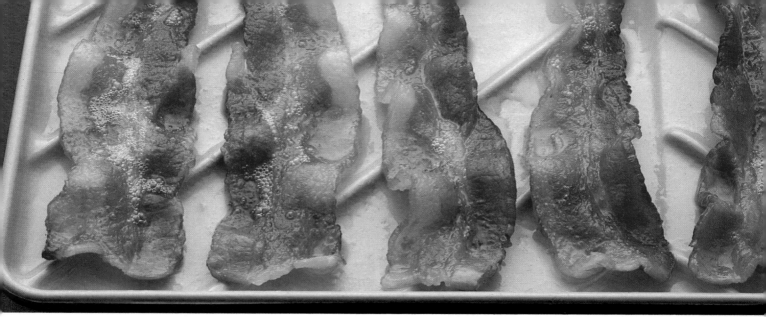

Refrigerated Meat Chart

Item	Preparation	Microwave Instructions
Bacon	1. Arrange bacon on 3 layers of paper towels on oven floor or plate, or layer on roasting rack. Cover with another paper towel.	1. Microwave at **High.** 1 to 6 slices: **¾ to 1 min./slice** Over 6 slices: **½ to ¾ min./slice** 2. Remove from oven. Bacon will still look slightly underdone. 3. Let stand 5 minutes. Bacon will be cooked after standing.
Canadian Bacon Slices ¼ in. thick	1. Arrange on serving plate in single layer. Cover with wax paper.	1. Microwave at **High.** Rotate after half the time. 2 slices: **¾ to 1¼ minutes** 4 slices: **1½ to 2½ minutes** 8 slices: **3 to 3½ minutes**
Fully Cooked Prepared Sausages Frankfurters, Knockwurst, Bologna	1. Arrange sausages on plate. Puncture large sausages twice with fork. Cover with wax paper. If heated in bun, wrap sausage and bun in a paper towel.	1. Microwave at **High.** Turn over and rearrange after half the time. Medium Sausages: 1 sausage: **½ to ¾ minutes** 2 sausages: **¾ to 1¼ minutes** 4 sausages: **1¾ to 2¾ minutes** Large Sausages: 1 sausage: **¾ to 1¼ minutes** 2 sausages: **1¼ to 1¾ minutes** 4 sausages: **2 to 3 minutes**
Canned Ham 1 to 12 lbs.	1. Place ham in 12 × 8-in. baking dish. Cover loosely with plastic wrap. 2. Estimate total cooking time at **6 to 8 minutes per lb.**	1. Microwave at **50% (Medium)** for half the estimated time. Turn over; recover. Insert probe or microwave thermometer through plastic wrap so tip is in center of meat. 2. Microwave at **50% (Medium)** remaining time, or until internal temperature is 130°. Let stand, tented with foil, 5 to 10 minutes.

Delicatessen & Fast Foods

The deli section of your supermarket, fast food shops and take-out restaurants provide a wide variety of fully prepared foods to heat and eat. Some are packaged in heat-retaining containers, while others are sold from a refrigerated case. Microwaving time depends on the starting temperature as well as the quantity of food. If the food has been refrigerated in the store or at home, it will take longer to bring it to serving temperature. If it has only cooled to room temperature, it will take less time. Follow directions in the charts carefully.

Reheating Fast Food Sandwiches Chart

Item	Amount	Microwave Time at High: Room Temp.	Microwave Time at High: Refrigerated	Procedure
Hamburgers				
Single	1	¼-½ min.	¾-1½ min.	Follow photo directions, opposite.
	2	½-1½ min.	1-3 min.	
Double	1	¼-¾ min.	¾-2½ min.	Follow photo directions, opposite.
	2	¾-1½ min.	1¼-4 min.	
Triple	1	½-¾ min.	1¾-3 min.	Follow photo directions, opposite.
	2	1-1¼ min.	2¼-4½ min.	
Fish Sandwiches	1	¼-¾ min.	¾-1½ min.	Follow photo directions, opposite.
	2	½-1 min.	1-1¾ min.	
Chicken Sandwiches	1	¼-¾ min.	1-1½ min.	Follow photo directions, opposite.
	2	¾-1 min.	1½-2 min.	
Turkey Sandwiches	1	½-¾ min.	½-1 min.	Follow photo directions, opposite.
	2	¾-1 min.	1-2 min.	
Roast Beef Sandwiches	1	½-1 min.	1-1¼ min.	Follow photo directions, opposite.
	2	1-1½ min.	1-2 min.	
Ham & Cheese Sandwiches	1	¾-1 min.	1-1½ min.	Follow photo directions, opposite.
	2	1¼-2 min.	1½-2½ min.	
Enchiladas, Burritos	1	¾-1 min.	1¼-1¾ min.	Remove original wrapper. Wrap in paper toweling. Place on serving plate. Microwave until warm to touch.
	2	1-1½ min.	2-2½ min.	
Corn Dogs	1		½-1 min.	Place on paper towel or paper towel-lined plate. Rearrange after half the time.
	2		1-2 min.	
	4		1½-2½ min.	

How to Reheat Fast Food Sandwiches

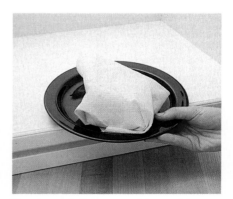

Room Temperature. If sandwich has not been refrigerated, leave it in container with top open, or remove from container and wrap in paper toweling. Microwave at High as directed in chart, opposite, until warm to the touch.

Refrigerated Temperature. Remove refrigerated sandwich from container. Remove top of bun and lettuce. Place bottom half of sandwich on paper towel-lined plate. Microwave at High as directed in chart until warm to touch.

Replace lettuce and top of bun. Wrap sandwich in paper towel. Microwave at High 20 to 30 seconds. When heating 2 sandwiches, rearrange after half the time.

Reheating Delicatessen & Fast Foods Chart

Item	Amount	Microwave Time at High: Room Temp.	Microwave Time at High: Refrigerated	Procedure
Fried Chicken Fully Cooked	1 piece	¼-¾ min.	¾-1 min.	Place pieces on paper towel-lined plate or baking dish. Cover with another paper towel. For 2 or 4 pieces, rotate after half the time. For 9 to 15 pieces, rotate dish and rearrange pieces after half the time.
	2 or 3 pieces	1-1½ min.	1¼-1½ min.	
	4 pieces	1-1¾ min.	1½-3 min.	
	9 pieces	1½-2 min.	3½-4 min.	
	15 pieces	3-6½ min.	5-8 min.	
Pizza Regular or Deep Dish	10- to 12-in. pizza	70% (Med.-High): 3-8 min.	70% (Med.-High):	Place in oven on cardboard base or on paper towel-lined plate. Microwave until heated and cheese is bubbly.
Thin Crust	1 piece	15-30 sec.	¾-1¼ min.	
	2 pieces	20-40 sec.	1-1¾ min.	
Thick Crust	1 piece	20-40 sec.	½-1½ min.	
	2 pieces	25-45 sec.	¾-3 min.	
Barbecue Ribs or Braised Ribs	⅓ to ½ lb.		2-4 min.	Arrange in 8×8-in. baking dish so pieces are not overlapping and meatiest portions are toward the outside. Cover with plastic wrap. Microwave until heated, rearranging pieces after half the time.
	⅔ to 1 lb.		3-5 min.	
Stuffed Pork Chops ¾ lb. each	1		50% (Med.) 4-6 min.	Arrange on serving plate or in baking dish. Cover with plastic wrap. Microwave until heated, rotating dish 2 or 3 times and rearranging chops after half the time. Let stand, covered, 3 minutes.
	2		8-10 min.	
	4		12-15 min.	
Egg Rolls 2 oz. each.	1		¾-1 min.	Place on paper towel-lined plate. Microwave until heated, rotating dish or rearranging rolls after half the time.
	2		1¼-1½ min.	
	4		2½-3 min.	

Item	Amount	Microwave Time at High: Room Temp.	Microwave Time at High: Refrigerated	Procedure
Meat Loaf	¾ lb.		7-10 min.	Place on serving plate. Cover with plastic wrap. Microwave until heated, rotating every 3 minutes. Let stand, covered, 5 minutes.
Meatballs in Sauce	1 pint 1 quart		3-6 min. 6-8 min.	Place in 1-qt. casserole; cover. Microwave until sauce is very hot, stirring every 3 minutes. Let stand, covered, 5 minutes.
Salisbury Steak ⅓ lb. each	1 2		1½-2 min. 3-5 min.	Place on serving plate. Cover with plastic wrap. Microwave until heated, turning over and rotating after half the time.
Chinese Main Dishes Chow Mein, Fried Rice, Sweet & Sour Pork, Pepper Steak, Sukiyaki	Pints or quarts	1-4 min.	2-7 min.	Place in 1-qt. casserole. Microwave until heated, stirring 2 or 3 times during cooking.
Stuffed Cabbage Rolls ½ lb. each	1 2 4		4-6 min. 6-10 min. 10-14 min.	Place rolls in casserole or baking dish. Cover with plastic wrap. Microwave until heated, rotating dish 3 or 4 times and rearranging rolls after half the time.
Stirrable Casseroles Baked Beans, Goulash, Stroganoff, Macaroni & Cheese	1 pint 1 quart		4-5 min. 6-8 min.	Place in 1-qt. casserole; cover. Microwave until heated, stirring 2 or 3 times during cooking.
Fruit Pie	1 slice 2 slices		¾-1 min. 1½-2½ min.	Place on serving plate. Microwave until warm, rearranging after half the time.

Index